What the experts say:

'Michael Cox has written the most important book to [illegible] Cold War American foreign policy. It combines a comprehensive overview of the subject with a complex interpretation of the domestic roots of and international constraints on American policy. It will be required reading for anyone trying to understand the international role of the last remaining superpower at the close of the century.'

– BENJAMIN SCHWARZ, SENIOR EDITOR DESIGNATE, WORLD POLICY JOURNAL, NEW YORK, FORMERLY RAND

'A splendid account of recent US foreign policy. Michael Cox shows both the surprising continuities after the Cold War as well as the dramatic shifts from geopolitics to geo-economics. Examining US actions in all areas of the globe, Cox succinctly and incisively evaluates the surprising strengths as well as the major shortcomings of recent American diplomacy. As the 1996 American elections approach, there is no better book to read on Clinton's foreign policies.'

– MELVYN P. LEFFLER, EDWARD STETTINIUS PROFESSOR OF AMERICAN HISTORY, UNIVERSITY OF VIRGINIA

'This is a clear-headed and thoughtful assessment of the increasingly coherent way the US is devising, in a tumultuous period, a recrafted foreign policy to construct a global system in which democratic capitalism and a growing global economy can flourish while the US remains the dominant actor. Although researched and written at a time when orthodox opinion portrayed Clinton's administration as indecisive innocents, Cox's conceptual analysis is robust enough to hold good even after the progress towards Middle East and Bosnian peace agreements is starting to transform that perception. Cox has looked well beyond the headlines to produce the most comprehensive and far-sighted study of this confusing topic so far.'

– MARTIN WALKER, US BUREAU CHIEF, THE GUARDIAN, AND SENIOR FELLOW, WORLD POLICY INSTITUTE, NEW SCHOOL FOR SOCIAL RESEARCH, NEW YORK

US Foreign Policy after the Cold War

CHATHAM HOUSE PAPERS

The Royal Institute of International Affairs, at Chatham House in London, has provided an impartial forum for discussion and debate on current international issues for 75 years. Its resident research fellows, specialized information resources, and range of publications, conferences, and meetings span the fields of international politics, economics, and security. The Institute is independent of government.

Chatham House Papers are short monographs on current policy problems which have been commissioned by the RIIA. In preparing the papers, authors are advised by a study group of experts convened by the RIIA, and publication of a paper indicates that the Institute regards it as an authoritative contribution to the public debate. The Institute does not, however, hold opinions of its own; the views expressed in this publication are the responsibility of the author.

CHATHAM HOUSE PAPERS

US Foreign Policy after the Cold War

Superpower Without a Mission?

Michael Cox

Pinter
A Cassell Imprint
Wellington House, 125 Strand, London WC2R 0BB, United Kingdom

First published in 1995

British Library Cataloguing in Publication Data
A CIP catalogue record for this book is available from the British Library

ISBN 1-85567-221-9 (Paperback)
1-85567-220-0 (Hardback)

Typeset by Koinonia Limited
Printed and bound in Great Britain by
Biddles Limited, Guildford and King's Lynn

Contents

Acknowledgments

All books accumulate intellectual and personal debts, and this one is no exception. First, I would like to thank the Japanese National Institute for Research Advancement (NIRA) in Tokyo for its generous funding for this project. I also wish to thank all those who participated in the Chatham House study groups associated with the writing of this volume – in particular Professor Jack Spence and Professor Sir Laurence Martin. Special thanks are extended to Edmund Ions, who participated in the project in its early days; at Chatham House, to Margaret May for her editorial guidance, as well as to Marie Ciechanowska and Hannah Doe; and to numerous US government officials who gave of their time and expertise in interviews conducted in both London and Washington. My former colleagues at the Department of Politics at the Queen's University of Belfast also deserve a particular mention for their help and support over the past few years. Finally, a special word of appreciation must go to my children – Ben, Dan, Nell and Annaliese – and to my wife Fiona, to whom this book is dedicated, and without whom it would have been inconceivable.

Aberystwyth, September 1995 M.C.

Chapter 1

Introduction

> 'The passing of the Cold War, in presenting us a world which appears to be devoid of anything that could be seen as a major great-power enemy of this country, also obviously presents us with a problem for which few of us are prepared'
>
> – GEORGE KENNAN[1]

In the context of a wide-ranging discussion about the US presidential election of 1992, the American commentator Norman Ornstein asked a stunningly simple question – one which academic analysts, serious journalists, two American presidents and the author of this particular volume have been trying to answer since 1989: essentially what was a superpower like the United States actually 'supposed to do in a world no longer dominated by a superpower conflict'?[2] Ornstein tried but in the end failed to provide an adequate answer. Indeed, as he admitted, there might not even be one. The United States, he implied, had simply lost its bearings, with no guarantee it would ever rediscover the international road back to true happiness. Having lost an enemy to fight, the nation seemed to be all at sea in the new world; more secure than it had ever been in the twentieth century but without a mission to fulfil.[3]

This new world was of course one which many Americans had dreamed of but for which few had actually planned, least of all that most pragmatic of postwar presidents, George Bush. Even so, when it arrived, it provoked one of those great rolling debates of which intellectuals in the United States are especially fond. Now, however, the topic was not US decline – a favourite ever since the Vietnam war – or even that old perennial, how to avoid American overextension in an age of insolvency, but what to do in an international system in which the United States no longer had a fixed point of opposition around which to organize its affairs. The debate which this loss of a magnetic north provoked was generally intelligent and, until the election of the 104th Congress in November 1994, reasonably well-mannered as well. Moreover at first it gave the impression that for every question asked there was almost certainly an answer waiting to be discovered somewhere between the covers of *Foreign Affairs*. Yet as the discussion unfolded, one thing became abundantly clear. Nobody – not even the Council on Foreign Relations – seemed to have any easy answers.

Thus, while most analysts accepted that the United States should now be doing less abroad, few could specify exactly how much less. Indeed, as policy-makers began to think and act more selectively, some began to worry that the United States was perhaps doing too little and should be doing more. Again, while many believed that the UN should become the principal vehicle for US actions in the post-Cold War era, others argued – in increasingly large numbers – that the organization represented an obstacle to, rather than a useful medium for, the advancement of US interests. There were similar divisions concerning America's democratic 'mission'.[4] Many insisted, with almost Wilsonian passion, that with the passing of the USSR the United States now had the opportunity to complete the democratic revolution it had started after the First World War. Others tried to squash such fantasies, dismissing the whole notion as mere rhetoric. In the real world, they mused, such idealism was not only a poor guide to policy, but likely to lead to the same crusading moralism that had so distorted US foreign policy during the years of the Cold War.

There did not seem to be very much agreement either about the most basic issue of all: namely, what exactly constituted the American national interest and where was it supposed to lie in a post-Cold War world? Clearly, as Laurence Martin has pointed out, there was 'no reason why the defeat of the Soviet Union' should have meant 'an American withdrawal from world politics'.[5] Nonetheless, precisely because the Soviet Union had been defeated, certain areas of the world where the US had been involved before inevitably became less important. But how much less? This was a question to which there was no easy answer, as events in both ex-Yugoslavia and sub-Saharan Africa demonstrated. Here the United States apparently had no interests at all. But could it just leave these places to fester? Do as little or as much as the media – in the shape of CNN – demanded? Or accept that as world leader it had responsibilities (almost of a moral quality) which transcended the classic realist definition of interest? This was a genuine dilemma, and not surprisingly different analysts of the international scene came up with quite different solutions to it.

Intellectual disarray at one level mirrored what many saw, and still see, as policy confusion at another. Bush, it was generally agreed, had done a reasonably competent job in negotiating the conclusion of the Cold War in Europe, especially as regards Germany. However, his more ambitious project of realizing a new world order never really got off the ground – a victim on the one hand of the disintegration of the USSR (something he himself had actively tried to prevent), and on the other of a 'homeward-bound electorate' increasingly disinclined to become entangled in other people's affairs. Bill Clinton, according to his numerous critics, has fared no better. Indeed, if one were to accept even half of what has been said about him, it would appear that Clinton – perhaps one of the least respected American presidents this century – has not only failed to provide an answer to Ornstein's original question, but does not even seem to understand what the question means. The result, we have been informed by pundits inside and outside the USA, has been a series of foreign policy fiascos ranging from Somalia through Bosnia to China, and concluding with what some argue has been his disastrous policy of appeasing Yeltsin. In fact, Clinton's foreign policy has, according to his many enemies, been so confused that he has managed to make his less than visionary predecessor look like a world-class statesman.[6]

The notion that US foreign policy since the end of the Cold War has become increasingly incoherent has been repeated so often in learned journals, by those sidelined by the end of the Cold War, as well as by newspaper editors trying to sell more copy, that it is now regarded as self-evident and virtually unchallengeable. But that is precisely what this book sets out to do: not because I am looking for intellectual confrontation for its own sake, but because my research for this volume does not incline me to the standard conclusion that US policy has been quite as confused as has been suggested.[7] This is not to underestimate US foreign policy problems since the disappearance of that most useful of threats, the Soviet Union. Indeed, as I shall endeavour to show, living without a clear and discernible challenge to its interests has created immense problems for the United States. But it is important to maintain a sense of balance and proportion. Sweeping generalizations about US foreign policy failures and setbacks are no substitute for concrete analysis of the way or ways in which the United States has tried to come to terms with post-Cold War realities – sometimes more successfully and intelligently than many critics would have us believe.

This brings me, logically, to my second argument. Generally speaking, those critical of the way things have gone over the past few years have tended to see the problem in essentially subjective terms, the implication being that if only the US had different leaders with different ideas who paid more attention to what was going on in the world, then all might be well. This line of argument is both empirically misleading and conceptually naive.[8] For where problems have arisen they have done so, in my view, less because of poor judgment, a lack of vision or a failure to see the whole picture – three of the standard charges directed against Clinton, in particular – than because the world has become a far more complicated and less manageable place: in part because of the end of the Cold War, but also because of great and irreversible tectonic shifts in the balance of world economic and political power which make it extremely difficult for policy-makers to come up with easy solutions or unambiguous answers to the problems they confront on an everyday basis. In fact, blaming policy-makers in general, or Clinton in person, for failing to devise clearer, more effective policies is rather like blaming the messenger because one does not like the message: the message in this particular case being that the international system has become an increasingly complex arena with many more actors who are simply not prepared any longer to follow the United States or submit to its demands. How much easier life must have been for the wise men of American foreign policy back in 1947 when the US controlled half of the world's economy, faced no serious economic competition and was the sole possessor of the atomic bomb. Certainly, there must be one or two policy-makers at the CIA in Langley, in the State Department at Foggy Bottom or across the way at the Pentagon who would gladly swap their situation for that of their predecessors back in those halcyon days of the early Cold War when America was a true superpower.

Those who would criticize policy-makers also seem to show a remarkable lack of awareness of how difficult it is to develop a coherent foreign policy in the United States. The US is an 'exceptional' country in many respects – in its constitutional complexity, in its ethnic diversity, in its commitment to a higher democratic purpose, and in the degree to which domestic pressures and forces have invaded the space normally occupied by what we call 'foreign' policy. Some might wish that it were different. But the fact remains that the United States not only inhabits a complex international system but has a turbulent political system of its own; one which has become even more turbulent and less structured since the end of the Cold War. Thus if there is confusion, it stems less from those who make policy and more from a decentred and highly fragmented system which places enormous demands and imposes such constraints on its policy-makers. The wonder is that US foreign policy has been as coherent as it has since the fall of the Berlin Wall.

Finally, all those who complain about policy incoherence in the post-Cold War era forget two rather important points. The first, quite simply, is that US policy during the Cold War was equally contradictory. Indeed, reading through the list of misdemeanours committed by American policy-makers over the past few years one might easily be forgiven for thinking that there had been a smooth policy ride from the Truman Doctrine, through Korea and Vietnam, to the almost totally unexpected collapse of Soviet power in Eastern Europe in 1989. Nothing could be further from the truth.[9] Secondly, many of the broader objectives sought by the United States since 1989 actually bear a strong resemblance to those it pursued before the end of the Cold War and the fall of the USSR. Admittedly the geopolitical context has altered. But the underlying aim of the US – to create an environment in which democratic capitalism can flourish in a world in which the US still remains the dominant actor – has not significantly altered. Analysts seem to have become so attached to the idea that everything has changed since the fall of communism that they sometimes forget there is a great deal which has not. There is much about our new world order which is not really 'new' at all. The following chapters attempt to show how this is true across the whole arena of US foreign policy.

Chapter 2 looks at the United States itself. To make sense of American foreign policy one must, as I have already suggested, examine the way the American system works. After a brief analysis of the way foreign policy was constructed during the Cold War, I discuss some of the critical changes since the collapse of communism, in particular the growing role of Congress and conversely the declining power of the president. The chapter concludes with an examination of foreign policy reform, and a discussion of that age-old problem: whether or not the United States is likely to go, or has already gone, isolationist.

Chapter 3 examines foreign economic policy. With the passing of the Cold War the American definition of security has radically changed – away from its previous focus on strategic issues towards matters such as trade and competitiveness. The implications of this paradigmatic shift are assessed in some detail.

Chapter 4 addresses more traditional military questions which some rather naively assumed would go away once the Cold War had come to an end. After looking at the records of both the Bush and the Clinton administrations the chapter considers Clinton's critics, both liberal and conservative, examines the increasing importance of nuclear non-proliferation as a foreign policy issue, and asks whether or not the US will be able to sustain a viable nuclear non-proliferation regime while still retaining its own nuclear arsenal. The chapter concludes with a discussion of the impact of declining military budgets upon American society.

Chapter 5 looks at the very serious efforts made by the Clinton administration to construct what it hoped would one day become a new strategic alliance with Russian reform. The chapter analyses developments in Russia since 1992 and explains why these have led some Americans at least to doubt the wisdom of Clinton's original policy. It suggests that, although the Clinton administration has been forced by events to modify its strategy, there are good reasons to believe that the United States will continue to work with Russia as long as Russia does not altogether abandon the path of economic and political reform.

Chapter 6 assesses how well the United States has adapted to the new environment in Europe. After analysing US policy under Bush and Clinton, it assesses the old special relationship with Britain (and the new one with Germany), then looks at the issue of NATO expansion, and concludes with a discussion about whether or not America and Europe are bound for separation.

Chapter 7 examines the Asia-Pacific: a region of immense and growing importance where the United States has found it especially difficult to fashion a consistent policy since the end of the Cold War. The somewhat revisionist thesis advanced here is that many of the dilemmas now confronting the United States in the region are less the result of poor judgment (though there has obviously been some) and more the consequence of the long-term success of its policies since the end of the Second World War. These issues are explored through an analysis of US relations with four very different countries: Japan, China, North Korea and Vietnam. The chapter concludes with an assessment of US attempts since 1993 to create something which as yet does not exist – a developed Pacific Rim community.

In Chapter 8 we look at the Third World: a term that was once a utopian statement of intent by the less developed countries, but now one whose very meaning is disputed by analysts. After briefly considering the impact of the Cold War upon the Third World, the chapter assesses what the collapse of communism has meant for regions as diverse as Africa, the Middle East, Latin America and South Asia, and finally focuses on how US policy has adjusted to post-Cold War realities, in particular over the problem of foreign aid.

In the conclusion I reflect on the future. As the United States approaches the millennium it has good reason to be confident. It is in a uniquely powerful military position. Its economy is still immensely productive. And its cultural 'star' is in the ascendant in a world now more open than at any time in the past. But in spite of all this (and here we return to one of the core arguments of the book) its ability to shape events is not what it was half a century ago. Furthermore, with the passing of the Cold War, it is clearly far less willing to take the risks involved, or pay the price normally associated with being an effective world leader. Some, quite reasonably, may applaud this development on the grounds that the country needs a breathing space to put its own house in order. Given America's past record, it might also be argued that there is a good deal to be said in favour of this particular superpower fighting shy of interfering in the internal affairs of other people's countries. But one does not have to worship at the altar of history to know that when superpowers decline to play a superpower role, the outcome may be far from benign.

Chapter 2

The constrained superpower?

> 'Despite the logic of "realpolitik" and the desires of many politicians in practice, foreign and national security policy has never been insulated from domestic politics. The notion that politics stops at the water's edge is therefore more myth than reality, more prescription than description. Indeed, since the Vietnam War, and more recently the demise of Cold War rivalry, foreign and domestic politics have become apparently inseparable'
>
> — MAIDMENT AND MCGREW[1]

In a provocative study published only five years before the end of the Cold War, three respected analysts (one of whom went on to become Bill Clinton's adviser on national security affairs) drew the public's attention to what they believed had become one of the great issues facing the American Republic: the apparent difficulty it had in formulating a consistent foreign policy. This unfortunate situation had little or nothing to do with personality or ideology. Rather, it was suggested, the crisis flowed from the way in which international politics was actually formulated in the United States. Many of the distortions in the process could of course be traced back to the Vietnam war. But this was not all. Problems generated by partisan politics during the Cold War, an erosion in the authority of the foreign policy establishment and the increased irresponsibility of both Congress and the press, had also contributed to what the authors characterized as a 'foreign policy breakdown'. The situation was indeed critical, and while all three looked forward to more rational times, there was no mistaking their pessimism. Without profound reform, they argued, the United States was doomed to remain trapped in a political quagmire – quite literally its 'own worst enemy', as the title of their book suggested.[2]

The observation that American foreign policy had become an increasingly chaotic affair since that almost mythic, all-too-brief period in the late 1940s when intellectual giants apparently walked the land, was hardly an original one. No less a figure than George F. Kennan had written at great length about what he saw as the almost impossible task of the foreign service in the United States. According to Kennan, however, America was unable to construct a realistic strategy, not because of distortions in an otherwise rational democratic system, but because of the system itself. America, he concluded sadly, was simply not able, and probably not fit, to be a serious superpower. The United States, he argued, was, like man himself, a 'cracked vessel' where self-seeking politicians and an uninformed electorate combined in an almost unholy alliance to make impossible a genuine and informed debate about America's true purpose in the world.[3]

Now while we need not share Kennan's misanthropic world view, the much misundertood critic of the doctrine of containment does at least draw our attention to a much noted phenomenon: that making foreign policy in the United States has never been an easy task. Indeed, the structure of the American government virtually decrees that this should be so. As Edward Corwin has pointed out in his oft-repeated aphorism, the American Constitution, by its very nature, is an invitation to the two branches of government 'to struggle for the privilege of directing American foreign policy'.[4] Nor is this all. Other factors – the country's extraordinary ethnic diversity, the highly accessible character of the American political system, and the fact that the United States is a huge country facing three great continental land masses to its south, east and west – have also conspired to make life intensely complicated for those whose job it has been to establish a clear international agenda. Defining the national interest may seem perfectly easy to detached academics. Actually translating that idea into practice in a country so diverse, so turbulent, and so open and democratic is quite another matter.

In this chapter I explore these complex problems in a little more detail. In the first part I look, briefly, at foreign policy-making before the fall of Soviet power, arguing that the Cold War – in its own rather crude way – partially resolved some of the problems identified above. I then discuss why the end of the Cold War has made life more difficult for US foreign policy-makers, especially for American presidents. Next, I assess the implications of the mid-term elections of 1994, and suggest that the victory of the Republicans has opened up a critical new phase in that ongoing struggle between legislature and executive for control of America's foreign policy agenda. This is followed by a short look at foreign policy reform. I conclude with a discussion about whether or not the United States is going isolationist.

The Cold War consensus

For one so observant about US foreign policy during the Cold War, Kennan was remarkably unobservant about how well the system functioned for the better part of four decades. The exaggerated and simplified rhetoric of those years may have led to an overextension of American power. It clearly produced a rigidity in the foreign policy debate from which it proved almost impossible to escape. Nevertheless, the Cold War 'worked', and when it collapsed, a critical vacuum was left which neither George Bush nor Bill Clinton found easy to fill.

The first and most obvious way in which the Cold War 'worked' was in terms of resolving the ever-present tension between Congress and president in favour of the executive branch. As Michael Foley has pointed out, if Congress was the 'chief victim' of the Cold War, the presidency was its most obvious 'beneficiary'.[5] Naturally, this new situation did not of itself eliminate all of the tensions between the two. From the 1970s onwards, there was, as has often been noted, a revival of the age-old struggle over who, precisely, would shape America's international agenda. However, the outcome of this conflict was not as revolutionary as some have claimed. Basically, so long as the man in the White House appeared to be managing US relations with the rest of the world 'with at least moderate competence and success', the public continued to rally behind him.[6] In this way, and by virtue of his 'capacity to react to pressing needs with the appropriate speed, expertise, secrecy and unity of purpose', the President still retained 'a good deal of power and freedom to manoeuvre' in foreign policy matters.[7]

The Cold War thus helped overcome the ever-present tendency in the American government to inertia, confusion and stalemate. In the process it privileged the position of the President, who in a nuclear age represented and spoke for the nation as a whole. In fact the nuclear standoff itself further enhanced the power and prestige of the presidency. Only the President, after all, had access to the highly classified information regarding nuclear weapons. It was he in the end, and not Congress, who determined whether or not the United States was seriously threatened. And it was the President – and the President alone – who had the power to decide whether or not to launch a pre-emptive or retaliatory nuclear attack against the USSR. Given such awesome responsibilities, it was hardly surprising that the Constitution's invitation to struggle over the making of US foreign policy was decided in favour of the executive.

If the Cold War emphasized leadership over consultation, and allowed Presidents a degree of autonomy they were not permitted in the domestic field, it also helped focus the collective mind on wider international issues. For a nation with a long tradition of isolationism, this was no small achievement. Moreover, because of the Cold War, most Americans were generally willing to underwrite what was done abroad in their name. There were limits, of course. The overwhelming majority, obviously, wished to avoid war with Russia and, after Vietnam, were reluctant to support US military intervention overseas. Nevertheless, as long as they were convinced (which most of them were until the second half of the 1980s) that American interests were threatened by a totalitarian power whose goal was nothing less than world domination, they were prepared to pay a reasonable price – though not an exorbitant one – to support the cause of international stability.

Finally, the Cold War not only mobilized popular consent behind US foreign policy, but also made it possible for successive Presidents to demand (and normally get) most of what they wanted in order to advance America's goals in the world. Clearly, the US economy could not afford everything, as the fiscally conservative Eisenhower pointed out to his critics in the 1950s. Foreign policy-makers, moreover, could not ignore wider budgetary constraints. Yet in spite of this, the amount that went into national security was huge by any standards: approximately 70 per cent of the budget before the 1970s and over 20 per cent in an average year thereafter. These were not trifling sums. Indeed, it is remarkable that in one of the least dangerous decades of the Cold War (the last one following the Soviet invasion of Afghanistan) the United States expended well over a trillion dollars revitalizing containment and rebuilding its defences after a so-called 'decade of neglect'. Underwriting US power was an extemely expensive business, but so long as it was assumed that this was required in order to contain Soviet ambitions, then most Americans were prepared to shoulder the burden.

Foreign policy after the Cold War

The end of the Cold War upset all the rules of the international game and in the process altered the way Americans looked at the world. Symptomatically, perhaps, the first political victim of these profound changes was none other than the man who had led the United States to victory over the USSR. George Bush's defeat in 1992 was deeply significant. Here, after all, was a respected statesman who had negotiated the end of Soviet power and then organized the defeat of Saddam Hussein being rejected by the American people; and being rejected precisely because he was perceived as being a 'foreign policy' President. Moreover, having denied Bush a second term, Americans then decided to take a chance on an untested candidate like Bill Clinton, not because of his (almost non-existent) experience in international affairs, but for the opposite reason: because it looked as if he, unlike Bush, understood how to deal with America's pressing problems at home.

In effect, the 1992 election contained two important messages. The first, quite clearly, was that foreign policy left American voters cold in a world without the Soviet threat.[8] The second was that while the United States might still be a superpower, it would be a very different type of superpower until it had put its own house in order. America was not exactly abandoning the world – as we shall see. But it had lost its missionary zeal.[9]

The Bush defeat, therefore, was not just electorally interesting. In a more profound sense, it reflected an important shift in the electorate's view of America's real priorities in the post-Cold War world. This shift in turn was mirrored by another important change: in the nature of the relationship between American public opinion on the one hand and the foreign policy elite on the other. Let us recall that during the Cold War those who made policy were often able to manipulate images of the USSR so as to coax public opinion in a direction they wanted it to go. Paraphrasing Foley and Corwin, we might argue that before 1989 at least, policy-makers were the winners – and public opinion the losers – in the struggle over who determined foreign policy. With the disappearance of any observable threat to the United States, the tables were turned: since there was nothing 'external' left for policy-makers to manipulate, they found themselves having to follow public opinion, instead of being able to shape it.[10]

The first and most visible result of this change was that policy-makers became increasingly reluctant to engage in activities that might run counter to popular opinion; and in a situation where the US public appeared to have little stomach for foreign adventures, this made Bush and Clinton act all the more cautiously. The second result, it seemed, was to make the policy elite itself somewhat less strategic in its outlook. Bush was in fact the last president to try to construct some sort of 'doctrine' with his call for a new world order. Clinton was even more circumspect. Indeed, his appointment of the careful Warren Christopher and the pragmatic Anthony Lake to guide his foreign policy revealed a great deal about its character. Though both were heavily criticized for lacking vision, they were admirably suited to an age in which the American people were not looking for crusades to fight or fine visions about how to remake the world. In one sense, they were men whose time had arrived.

Clearly, the United States was not likely to be in an expansive mood in the post-Cold War era.[11] It was, however, in an increasingly parsimonious one. America, it was argued regularly, could not afford to be the world's chief policeman and underwriter. The Clinton administration then added its own economistic twist to this particular refrain. Now that economics had become its new god, it increasingly looked as if individual decisions about America's role in the world were just as likely to be determined by how much they cost (or by how much the United States might make out of them) as by whether or not they were wise. In a famous off-the-record speech in May 1993, Undersecretary of State Peter Tarnoff pointed out that the United States had neither the leverage, the inclination, nor (as he emphasized) 'the money' to solve all of the world's problems. Although his comments were officially repudiated, many saw them as providing a genuine insight into the Clinton administration's thinking about US foreign policy in an age of economic calculation.[12]

But perhaps the most important institutional consequence of the end of the Cold War was to redefine the position of the president within the political system. Without a Soviet threat, it certainly became increasingly difficult for the White House to rally popular support or bring an unruly legislature to heel. Furthermore, the need for a focal figure almost seemed to disappear with critical long-term implications for the policy-making process.

First, in the absence of strong leadership, policy-making became detectably less coherent as different sections of the foreign policy community vied with one another to impose their own particular views. As the power of the president to impose his own agenda diminished, interest groups also found it easier to set the international agenda. Thus what emerged as 'American' foreign policy was just as likely to be the result of pressure from below as of some well-thought-out strategy. Finally, as presidential authority declined, Congress, inevitably, became more important. In a world of nuclear confrontation the president quite simply had to be more than just *primus inter pares*. In a world of geo-economics, however, where the distinction between domestic and foreign policy became increasingly blurred, where the balance of trade was just as important as the balance of terror, and where counting jobs was as critical as counting Moscow's warheads, Congress was bound to play a larger role in defining American strategy. And how well it handled its new-found power would shape the future of both the country and the world.[13]

Congress resurgent

The end of the Cold War thus had a disturbing impact upon what had once been a relatively settled policy-making system. The result was to leave the United States floundering about for a purpose, Americans less inclined to get involved abroad, the position of the president more ambiguous in the field of foreign policy, and individual holders of that office less able to use their international role to enhance their position. Naturally, some continued to repeat the old truism that the executive still had what one analyst described as 'enormous leeway' in the area of foreign policy.[14] Formally speaking this was true. But there was no hiding the fact that in the new era the president's ability to set America's international agenda had diminished, and that while Congress may not have become the new 'King' as a result, it clearly had acquired greater influence.

The almost irresistible rise of Congress in the post-Cold War period assumed a particularly dramatic form when the Republicans seized control of both the Senate and the House of Representatives in November 1994.[15] Tapping many of the same sources of economic insecurity and resentment that had brought Clinton to the White House only two years earlier, the new Grand Old Party (GOP) clearly saw itself involved in a war to save the American people: from the sins of liberalism, from high taxes, from welfare scroungers and, most important of all, from unbalanced budgets.[16] Indeed, the main driving force behind the Republicans, Newt Gingrich, perceived the party's so-called 'Contract with America' as a binding mandate upon the party to change the course of history. The 104th Congress, he argued, was not being sent to Washington 'just to set records of legislative activity'. Rather it had been elected to 'renew American civilization'; to build what Gingrich termed 'a true civil society'.[17]

The 'Contract with America' was extremely vague about foreign policy and national security, the Republicans no doubt judging that these were not areas of great concern to the American people (and certainly not vote winners).[18] For this reason many at first concluded that their victory would make very little difference to the foreign policy debate. Some commentators even consoled themselves with the thought that although the new right within the Republican party was extremely vocal, the party's essential core of realists and internationalists – led by such stalwarts as Bob Dole, the Senate Majority Leader, Benjamin Gilman, the new chairman of the House International Relations Committee, and Richard Lugar – would guide the GOP away from the siren calls of isolationism and conservative radicalism. Thus while there might be 'major fights on marginal issues', as one analyst put it, there would be only 'marginal' scraps about really important questions.[19]

There may have been something in this. Nevertheless, it would have been foolish to underestimate the significance of November 1994. While the 'Contract' may not have provided a coherent strategic alternative, it did signal the beginning of a concerted and serious effort by the Republicans to gain virtual control over the national security agenda. Though criticized by some as being constitutionally improper, in many ways their attempt to seize the high ground was really only another (albeit more extreme) manifestation of that long historic struggle between the two branches of government to decide who would make foreign policy. Congress was now in a much stronger position to press its case.

The incipient challenge by the Republicans soon manifested itself with the publication of their *National Security Revitalization Act*. This dealt with a range of issues from missile defence to the United Nations, from who should command US forces to the thorny problem of NATO expansion. The Act was significant, however, not just in terms of what it said, what it proposed to cut (foreign aid), and what it also happened to support (such as military spending), but above all, perhaps, in terms of what it represented.[20]

The Act probably constituted one of the most direct attempts by Congress in the post-Cold War period to wrest control of foreign policy away from the executive. Though ostensibly designed to 'revitalize the national security of the United States', its real aim was to weaken the power of the White House. Clearly, a great deal was at stake, as Warren Christopher and William Perry pointed out in a damning critique. The proposed piece of legislation, they declared, was wrong in both content and conception, and would weaken, rather than enhance, US influence around the world. Not only that: if the Act went through, it would effectively destroy the 'authority' of the president to 'protect the national security and interests' of the nation. For all these reasons Clinton had to veto the proposed legislation. Indeed, if he did not, 'it would undermine this and every future president's ability to safeguard America's security'. In 'its present form' the Act simply had to be rejected.[21]

Another critic put the point even more bluntly. By its very proposal of the Act, the 104th Congress was simply 'butting in' where it had neither any 'business' nor any 'real expertise'.[22] Naturally enough, this was not a view shared by the Republicans. In their opinion, they not only had the appropriate capability, but more accurately reflected what the people actually wanted. Americans, they insisted, were opposed to foreign aid.[23] They did not want to waste money on the UN; and they were certainly not prepared to allow US troops to serve under foreign nationals. This might not have been something the State Department wanted to hear. The 'Contract with America' may have also been, as one commentator implied, a breach of contract with the rest of the world.[24] But there was no mistaking the message delivered in late 1994. America would come 'first' in the new world order.

The perestroika of American foreign policy

The noisy political struggle being conducted in public should not obscure the quieter debate which was going on within the elite itself about how to reorganize American foreign policy. Naturally enough there was some resistance to change. Many, for instance, took the view that one should leave well alone. Others reasoned that although the United States had slain the Soviet dragon, the international jungle was still teeming with thousands of snakes – any one of which could inflict a great deal of pain. It would therefore be foolish to introduce major changes into the way foreign policy was organized.

George Bush and to a lesser degree Bill Clinton appeared to agree with this line of analysis. Bush in particular was extremely wary of altering the foreign policy system. Yet neither he nor his successor could ignore the fact that the world had been turned upside down, and as a result changes would have to be introduced.

The first and perhaps most important reform of the US foreign policy process was to be financial, with large cuts in the national security budget. This trend had of course begun in the mid-1980s, but with the collapse of Soviet power, the pressure to economize increased enormously. The military was hit particularly hard (though whether it was hit hard enough will be analysed in Chapter 4). However, by 1995 the Department of Defense's real purchasing power was 30 per cent less than it had been a decade before. By the year 2000, moreover, defence spending was planned to be just over 3 per cent of US GNP – only the fourth largest item in the American budget – after social security, human services, and interest payments on the national debt.[25]

But defence was not the only area to feel the post-Cold War squeeze. Clinton was especially determined to bring down costs, and set about reducing the international affairs budget from more than $32bn in 1993 to $17bn in 1996. The US Agency for International Development (USAID) was also earmarked for cuts, and by the end of his first term was set to lose 21 of its foreign posts. The State Department proposed the elimination (or at least merger with itself) of three key agencies: AID itself, the United States Information Agency (USIA), and the Arms Control and Disarmament Agency (ACDA). After weeks of intense lobbying and infighting, Vice-President Al Gore finally turned down the proposal. There was little doubt, however, that the pressure to cut costs would continue.[26]

Cutting costs was just one of the ways in which the United States started to adjust to new world realities. Another was to increase the efficiency and enhance the status of that part of the policy apparatus whose main purpose was to improve US economic performance in the world. Here Clinton proved to be far more innovative than Bush (as we shall see in Chapter 3). For example, he created the National Economic Council (NEC) in 1993 under the direction of the Wall Street financier Robert E. Rubin, who later replaced Lloyd Bentsen as Secretary of the Treasury. Though primarily designed to coordinate foreign and domestic economic policies, one of the goals of the NEC, clearly, was to counter-balance the bureaucratic weight of the National Security Council (NSC) with its focus on more 'traditional' foreign and security policy concerns.[27] Another change, of perhaps even greater long-term importance, was the quite conscious attempt by Clinton to enhance the role of the Commerce Department under the dynamic leadership of the immensely influential Ron Brown, the former chairman of the Democratic Party. Almost overnight, his department, once a relatively insignificant force in foreign policy debates, moved centre-stage. Significantly, perhaps, while the reputation of others associated with the broad international goals of the Clinton administration declined after 1992, that of Ron Brown did not.

A final foreign policy reform worth mentioning here concerns the Central Intelligence Agency. The end of the Cold War had left the CIA in a somewhat exposed position. It was taken to task for having failed to anticipate the collapse of Soviet power. It then suffered a further humiliation when it was discovered that its whole operations in the former USSR and Russia had been compromised for ten years by a CIA employee, Aldrich Ames. Moreover, the organization as a whole, under its Director R. James Woolsey (who was forced to resign in early 1995), had no more than a cool relationship with Clinton's closest foreign policy advisers on the NSC. Evidently all was not well at Langley.[28]

It was Congress, however, that in the end came to the conclusion that the CIA was unable to chart its course in the post-Cold War world, and that in September 1994 created an independent commission to rethink the Agency's role. Despite active opposition by the CIA itself, as well as passive resistance from the White House, the commission was given the broadest possible mandate to propose changes in the structure, the power, the budget and indeed in the very existence of the Agency. Congress, in another assertion of its prerogatives, was, as one analyst noted at the time, literally 'forcing the CIA to become something like a company undergoing a court-supervised bankruptcy reorganization'.[29] Where the reorganization would actually lead was unclear. Many in fact feared that it might lead nowhere, like previous attempts to reform the Agency. However, there was a feeling (even shared by the Agency itself) that the organization had to change more than it had done already. Almost like Britain in the late 1950s, the CIA had lost an empire (to fight) but had still not found a proper role.[30]

Towards isolationism?

Will the United States go, or indeed has it already gone isolationist? The question has been asked many times before, and for good reason, given America's history and geography. In fact, many commentators seem to assume that isolationism is almost the natural condition of the United States and thus conclude that, with the Cold War over, the country will inevitably return to this more 'normal' state – with possibly disastrous consequences for the rest of the world.

The evidence supporting the isolationist thesis is powerful enough. Indeed, if the elections to the 104th Congress are to be taken as an accurate measure of popular feeling, Americans are not merely retreating towards isolationism, but are literally stampeding back into the laager from which they were forced to emerge in 1941. Sidney Blumenthal, among others, has advanced this particular argument with great force, and of all modern writers has probably drawn the most pessimistic conclusions from the 'electoral earthquake' of 1994. The mid-term elections, he argues, shattered a 'foreign policy consensus' that had held 'for more than half-a-century'. From Pearl Harbor to the early 1990s Americans had been basically internationalist in outlook; the 1994 results changed all that and forced internationalism onto the defensive. 'Anti-internationalist fevers' now 'wrack the body politic', he believes, leaving internationalists more isolated and demoralized than they have been for years. He concludes that internationalism is under 'a mounting assault' and there is no guarantee that it can ever be reconstituted in modern America.[31]

Blumenthal's pessimism reflects a widespread view that isolationism – or what he prefers to call negativity towards internationalism and all forms of multilateralism – has gained the upper hand in the United States. Some care does need to be exercised here, however, before we jump to this familiar and no doubt obvious conclusion.

First, although the 'isolationist strain' has clearly become far more powerful since the end of the Cold War, we should not necessarily draw the conclusion that Americans are completely opposed to the United States playing any role in world affairs. As one survey has shown, while Americans might not want to shed their blood or spend their money on what they see as worthless military adventures, on some issues (and in some areas) they would be prepared to support American action – if it were deemed to be vital to the defence of the national interest.[32]

Secondly, there is evidence to suggest that Americans still have a high regard for certain international institutions. A December 1994 survey by *Time Mirror*, for example, found that 60 per cent of those polled continued to support the NATO alliance. Earlier surveys even indicated a positive attitude towards the much criticized United Nations. Other polls conducted by the government also pointed to less grim conclusions than those reached by Blumenthal.[33]

Finally, nearly all Americans are aware (or have been made aware) that the United States is irretrievably locked into a world economy from which there can be no escape. Indeed, by repeating this truism almost *ad nauseam* since he became president, Clinton may have done more than any other single politician to counter the potential drift to isolationism over the past few years. Whether the drift can be halted is still not known. However, by telling his fellow citizens in no uncertain terms that the

United States has to compete in world markets or go under, he has performed two valuable services: to educate Americans in the facts of economic life; and to stem what could have become (and might still develop into) a self-destructive political tide – one which would hurt not only the United States, but the rest of the world as well.[34]

Chapter 3

From geopolitics to geo-economics? Competing in a global economy

'Ask not what your country can do
for you, ask what exporting can do
for your country and you.'
– *Business America*, 4 October 1993

One of the observations that has repeatedly been made about American foreign policy since the end of the Cold War is that its primary point of reference has gradually but perceptibly shifted: away from a concentration on more traditional security matters, to a new agenda in which the main preoccupation has not been to worry about 'the Soviet bear in the woods' – but to compete more effectively against allies who had once supported the United States in the struggle against communism. Indeed, according to this view, the United States had previously been unable to compete effectively because of the constraints imposed upon it by the superpower conflict. As the US Trade Representative Micky Kantor observed, prior to 1989 the United States had 'often neglected' its 'economic and trading interests because of foreign policy and defense concerns'.[1] But it would no longer be doing so, he argued, and henceforth would be pursuing its material goals without the Cold War compromising its economic interests.

Naturally enough, in this new environment, the rules of what Lester Thurrow termed the 'new game' were bound to change.[2] So too were US needs as it quickly became clear that America's main assets in the new world order were not so much rockets, tanks and warheads, as its trained workers, its educated entrepreneurs and its high-technology industries. Moreover, the object of the game now was not to prevent the spread of an alien ideology, but rather to maintain and where possible increase market share. This, however, did not make it any the less serious as a contest. For if the United States succeeded in 'winning' the economic battle it would mean domestic prosperity and continued influence abroad. But failure could easily lead to decline internationally and rising social tensions at home. The stakes in the post-communist era were every bit as high as they had been during the Cold War itself.[3]

This somewhat oversimplified picture obviously requires some qualification. Military power, after all, did not become completely irrelevant after the end of the Cold War. Nor had the United States been indifferent to economic questions before the demise of its main enemy. A powerful case could be made, in fact, that had it not been for American economic strength, containment might not have been successful. However, it was only with the withering away of the superpower conflict that policy-makers began to focus more completely on material questions – giving them the sort of attention that had previously been devoted to the 'Russian question'. Reagan and then Bush began the process. But it was really left to Clinton to take the process to its logical conclusion. Though developing policies already outlined in embryonic form by his predecessors, Clinton added to these to create a much criticized but ultimately quite novel geo-economic synthesis.[4]

This chapter explores the movement from an era of geopolitics to geo-economics by looking in detail at the record and role of the Clinton administration. The first part outlines Clinton's political economy. Next I examine some of the key figures who have helped set Clinton's economic agenda. This is followed by a consideration of some of the many practical implications of his approach, and finally of the problems involved with his international economic policies. Although they are relatively coherent, they do contain a number of contradictions which have not yet been fully resolved. Whether they will (or can) be remains an open question.

Clinton's political economy

One of the more enduring myths about Bill Clinton is that he came to power without a foreign policy. Nothing could be further from the truth. In fact, Clinton (like Ronald Reagan) assumed office with a fairly clear view of the world and the sort of policies he would have to pursue in order to enhance American power. Of course, unlike his neo-conservative predecessor, his main interest was not in the evil empire but in the world economy; and the principal means he hoped to use to mobilize

Americans behind his policies was not anti-communism but 'raw economic self-interest'.[5] Moreover, by linking the material aspirations of ordinary Americans to the pursuit of his wider economic goals, Clinton calculated that he would be able to counter any drift to isolationism. To this degree his call for America to 'compete, not retreat' had as much a political purpose as an economic one.[6]

Central to the Clinton administration's vision of America's new role in the world was the notion that in an era of geo-economics no distinction could be drawn between domestic politics and foreign policy. If the United States was not economically strong at home, he insisted, it was bound to be 'weaker abroad'. Nations that were 'stagnant', Clinton argued, lost 'the ability to finance military readiness, afford an activist foreign policy, or inspire allies by example'. The primary foreign policy task, therefore, was not to go out and perform miracles abroad, but instead to build the United States from the ground up through a series of well-coordinated economic measures – beginning with deficit reduction, continuing with a marked shift from defence spending to infrastructural investment in education and training, and moving forward over the longer term with government encouragement to key high-technology industries deemed to be vital to US power.

What Clinton referred to as a 'high-wage, high-growth economy' could not be built in isolation, however. From this perspective isolationism as a policy option made no sense whatsoever, especially for a nation that was more closely integrated into the world economy than at any time in its history. When one in seven American jobs was linked to trade, when US investments overseas amounted to several hundred billion dollars and when the country's future prosperity depended very directly upon the health of the international economy, the United States could hardly start thinking about distancing itself from the world. The real question for the Clinton administration, in fact, was not how to disentangle the United States from the international system, but rather, how to make itself a more competitive actor in it.[7]

From this logically flowed a renewed emphasis on successfuly competing in world markets. Increasing its share of world exports had always been one of America's goals (by the early 1990s it was selling annually well over $400bn worth of goods and services abroad). But now promoting trade almost seemed to become synonymous with US foreign policy itself. Nor was this a passing fad: it involved what one leading official called a 'change in mind set as significant as any that has taken place in [our] nation's history'. Indeed, in the new era, trade policy (according to

Jeffrey Garten) was now to be 'linked to virtually all aspects of American life: to jobs, to stable communities, to research and development programs, to new directions in education', even 'to health care reform where lower cost burdens on business [were] so important to competitiveness'.[8]

To be competitive, however, it was vital to rethink the relationship between government and business. For too long, according to the Clinton administration, US business had not received the support it needed or deserved – especially from the Republicans who for ideological reasons had been strongly opposed to the state being a major player in economic matters. But in a cut-throat world economy where governments in other countries were actively promoting business, the United States simply could not afford the luxury of *laissez-faire*. This might have been feasible when it had been economically preponderant, but was simply counterproductive when it was under serious economic challenge from both Europe and Japan. In this sense, the redistribution of economic power towards its main competitors during the 1970s and 1980s meant that America had no alternative but to construct a more intimate partnership between government and industry.[9]

Finally, Clinton's political economy rested upon an assumption that the United States had to be at the heart of a regionalized world economy. Though Clinton was building here on an agenda sketched out by Bush, he pursued this particular objective with much greater determination and purpose. He was certainly more forthright in public debate in explaining why achieving this goal was so critical for the United States. It would, he asserted, ensure continued US leadership of the world economic system; it would prevent any move by these regions towards self-sufficiency; and it would facilitate the movement towards a more open world economy upon which future US prosperity and influence depended.[10]

Economists in the White House

Many of Clinton's key appointments gave a clear indication of the sort of policies he might be pursuing during his first term. There was of course the usual sprinkling of lawyers and Wall Street financiers, including the powerful Robert Rubin. But many of his more interesting appointees came from the field of international economics, and a number were specialists in precisely those areas – trade access and competitiveness – that were to dominate the foreign policy agenda after 1992.

Perhaps the most commented-upon, and criticized, of Clinton's early appointments was Laura D'Andrea Tyson, whose 1992 study *Who's*

Bashing Whom? Trade Conflict in High-Technology Industries had already created an international stir. Tyson, who became Chair of the Council of Economic Advisers, never claimed that the main cause of US trade problems was unfair trading practices by other countries in general and Japan in particular. Rather, US problems, she insisted, were the logical consequence of 'flawed domestic choices'. She did claim, however (and this certainly had policy implications), that 'traditional approaches to trade and domestic policy' which had 'served the nation well when American companies had an unrivalled technological lead' were now 'no longer adequate'. Moreover, when faced with competitors who were playing by a different set of economic rules, the United States had to take decisive action, and devise what Tyson called new 'macroeconomic, trade and industrial policies' to promote America's high-technology industries.

This call for what amounted to managed trade and an industrial policy made Tyson's views unpopular among more conservative economists. They were even more upset by her somewhat sceptical attitude towards the efficacy of free markets. The market, she insisted, could not reverse America's economic fortunes. Indeed, the main conclusion of her influential study was that the United States simply could not 'afford the soothing but irrelevant position that market forces alone' could solve America's problems. A more interventionist approach would be necessary.[11]

Tyson's focus on high-technology trade conflict with Japan was partially mirrored in the acclaimed work of influential trade official Jeffrey Garten. In *A Cold Peace: America, Japan, Germany and the Struggle for Supremacy* (also published in late 1992) Garten concentrated on the new economic challenges facing the United States. Though more popular in presentation, and having as much to say about Germany as Japan, Garten's book agreed with Tyson that the threat facing the United States was now quite different from what it had been before. According to Garten, the country was confronted with important allies who were seriously challenging American economic hegemony; and all this in a context where the old rules about trade were breaking down. In this new era, America, he accepted, had been impelled to adopt a 'policy of managed trade'. But this did not appear to concern him so much as what he saw as the growing potential for 'cumulative economic tensions' between 'the big three' centres of power in the modern world economy. And without advocating an outright trade war against either Germany or Japan – most of his policy proposals were in fact designed to prevent such an outcome – he believed that the United States had to prepare itself for the economic battles ahead. In the new world order where economics was power (and American power by this definition was under challenge) the United States had to view trade issues in clear 'strategic terms'. In Garten's view it was entirely reasonable to pursue a more 'aggressive' and self-interested 'nationalist' line in economic matters. Indeed, only by doing so could the country's 'national economic strength' be significantly enhanced.[12]

The idea of economics as security was also the central theme in Theodore Moran's 1993 study *American Economic Policy and National Security*. Moran, who worked as Senior Adviser to the Policy Planning Staff during Clinton's first year, was possibly one of the most sombre analysts of the American economic scene.[13] The United States, he noted, faced at least three overlapping but 'conceptually distinct threats': a fundamental and cumulative economic decline relative to the other major industrial states; a loss of crucial economic and technological capabilities within the United States itself; and a growing dependence on other countries for vital goods. On these issues at least he was at one with Tyson. But unlike Tyson, Moran focused most of his analytic attention on proposals designed to bring about 'fundamental changes in American behaviour', rather than advocating what he termed 'neo-mercantilist policies' designed to shore up high-tech sectors or increase US trade access. He warned in fact against such policies, arguing that if the United States concentrated on getting short-term results instead of 'rebalancing America's mix of savings, consumption and investment', this could easily lead to a 'deterioration of the United States' international position'.

Finally, in this pantheon of economic influentials, one should include Clinton's close friend, and his Secretary of Labor, Robert Reich. Reich, who had previously taught business and public policy at Harvard, was the author of several books on political economy in which the dominant theme had been American economic decline and the main argument that new policies were required to reverse it.[14] Though by no means a consistent thinker, his influence upon the Clinton administration should not be underestimated. One idea of his in particular – globalization – played a crucial role in helping shape Clinton's economic outlook.

According to Reich the nation-state as an economic unit had lost a good deal of its meaning; there was effectively no such thing as a distinct or separate American economy. As he put it in a famous debate with Tyson, in the modern world market, 'us' no longer existed. The administration had some doubts about this proposition, but it did accept some of the implications of Reich's thesis. First, it agreed that if America was, as

Reich argued, a 'region' of a wider 'global economy', then it was quite impossible for the United States to escape from it. Isolationism was therefore economically inconceivable. It was also prepared to accept the equally Reichian notion that in the new global economy, inequality within nations was bound to increase. It was thus one of the tasks of government to address the social consequences of globalization and by so doing maintain an American sense of community. Finally, in this new order, where companies had 'no particular connection to any single nation', the duty of the state was not just to protect the weak, but also to help retrain those who were the victims of economic progress. If globalization was inevitable, as Reich insisted it was, then it was imperative that the Clinton administration worked out ways of ensuring that all Americans could partake of its benefits. This not only made good sociological sense (after all, no country wanted a large and potentially dangerous unskilled underclass inhabiting its cities), it also made economic sense insofar as it would guarantee America a better educated, and over the long term, a more productive workforce.[15]

Clinton and his critics

Viewed by their many critics as economic nationalists, and by others as old-style trade warriors willing to do anything to win markets for US goods, the members of the incoming Clinton team were undoubtedly the most economically focused ever to have come to office in the postwar period. Their concentration on creating more high-paid jobs inevitably made them popular with organized labour. However, they also received a fair amount of backing from US business, especially from those in high-technology industries or with major interests overseas. As one of Clinton's more vehement critics was forced to admit, by the time he took over from Bush, Clinton had more 'support from the business community than any Democrat since Johnson'.[16]

Clinton's assertive economic programme soon translated itself into policy. In his first month in office, for example, he threatened to block US sales to the government of European telecommunications and power-generated equipment, charging that the EC had conducted a 'buy-Europe' policy against American products. In January 1993 the United States ruled that Japan and eighteen other countries had been dumping steel products on the American market – a move condemned by the UK Department of Trade and Industry as 'outrageous harassment'. Additional moves were then contemplated against Europe and Japan, with the

US demanding 'results' from the latter while threatening the former with various sanctions if it did not open up its market to US goods and services. Naturally enough, Europe and Japan responded in kind; and by mid-1993 there was a fear in some quarters that the situation was fast getting out of hand.[17]

These concerns were mirrored in (and in part exacerbated by) a withering barrage of press criticism directed against Clinton's trade policies. In early 1993, for instance, the *New York Times* complained of a 'growing tension in trade relations' caused, in its view, by the President's 'new and more confrontational approach'. The *Wall Street Journal* (no friend of the Democrats) then accused the administration of caring 'less about principle than about making a political deal'. *The Economist*, not surprisingly, was even more scathing. Washington's approach, it asserted, was 'at best incompetent and at worst a step down the slippery path towards protectionism'. One noted British admirer of the United States (though not of Clinton) actually went so far as to suggest that the White House had been taken over by 'economic delinquents'. Writing in *The Financial Times*, Michael Prowse roundly condemned an administration which professed multilateralism in theory but in practice acted as 'judge and jury' on the world in general and the Japanese in particular. Prowse concluded that the United States was now being run by people who believed that the country was involved in some sort of 'race with Japan and the European Union' to determine who would be economically supreme in the twenty-first century. And he added, more in sorrow than in anger, that Clinton intended to 'take the gold'.[18]

The many charges levelled at Clinton reflected a combination of factors, including free-market opposition to a government which promised to play a more active role in economic affairs, a deep and abiding dislike by many of managed trade and, among his several foreign critics, a belief that Clinton was an old-fashioned imperialist who hoped (in the words of one journalist) to 'beat the world into economic submission'.[19] The most celebrated critique of Clinton's foreign economic policy, however, was penned by MIT economist Paul Krugman. In what many regarded as a seminal article published in *Foreign Affairs* in early 1994, Krugman took the administration to task not merely for attempting to gain comparable access to foreign markets, but for even being concerned with the question of competitiveness. The 'idea that a country's economic fortunes' were largely determined by its success on world markets was a 'hypothesis, not a necessary truth', according to Krugman. Thus the whole Clinton agenda was based on a false theoretical assumption. In

Krugman's view, moreover, the commitment to competitiveness was 'not only wrong but dangerous' and could easily skew domestic policies and threaten the very stability of the whole international economic system. A halt had to be called therefore to this new 'obsession': an obsession which in his opinion could easily lead to a 'wasteful spending of government money', 'bad public policy on a spectrum of important issues', and possibly 'protectionism and trade wars'.[20]

From NAFTA to the Uruguay Round

Clinton's various critics were extremely vocal. But in one area at least they had to concede that he was extraordinarily successful during 1993: namely in the promotion of the cause of world trade expansion. Indeed, in a series of really quite bold moves, Clinton pushed forward on at least three economic fronts during his first year in office. This led to the signing of the North American Free Trade Agreement (NAFTA) in November. In the same month Clinton then met with other leaders from the Pacific Rim in an attempt to breathe new life into Asia-Pacific Economic Cooperation (APEC). And after seven years' negotiation in the Uruguay Round, the General Agreement on Tariffs and Trade (GATT) was signed in Brussels in December. Taken together, the two agreements and the APEC summit constituted one of the great watersheds of the Clinton presidency; but it all began with NAFTA.[21]

NAFTA

NAFTA had many goals, not just the most obvious ones of increasing the volume of world trade and improving US access to the critical Mexican market (Mexico being America's fastest growing major export market, its second largest market for manufactured goods, and its third largest for agricultural products). Another main objective, clearly, was to institutionalize and, it was hoped, accelerate Mexico's continued transition towards a more open liberal market economy. This, it was reasoned, would promote political stability, which in turn would encourage a large inflow of new, as well as a return of old capital that had fled the country in the early 1980s. And, if things went according to plan, the new Mexico would act as a beacon and an inspiration for other Latin American countries; encouraging them to continue down the road to free-market capitalism, so destroying their left-wing, nationalist proclivities once and for all.

Having successfully negotiated NAFTA through Congress (going against a large section of his own party to do so) Clinton was now in a strong position to press ahead with the much larger GATT agreement. Between the NAFTA vote and the GATT signing, however, came APEC.

APEC

Though nowhere near as significant as NAFTA in the short term, it was hoped that APEC would one day evolve into something much more important. As Mickey Kantor noted, though most people had probably never heard of APEC before 1993 – it had held its first meeting in Australia in November 1989 – he wagered that this would change in the next few years. As it matured and developed it would, he argued, play several key roles, acting as a 'forum for consultations on trade policy' and as a vehicle through which the United States could encourage the expansion of trade and investment. As the fastest growing area in the world economy, and the number one export destination for American products, the United States could hardly ignore the Asia-Pacific. But it still needed an organization through which it could try to guide the region's destiny; and APEC was the chosen medium for this.[22]

In itself APEC had little immediate impact on the US trade position. But it did signal an American commitment to the wider cause of multilateralism in an area that was not only vital economically but undergoing critical political change. APEC also sent a warning shot across European bows, letting them know, in effect, that the United States had important economic interests in other parts of the world and that if Europe did not sign up to the forthcoming GATT there might be serious repercussions. One unnamed French Foreign Ministry official was clearly less than impressed by this American attempt to bully Europe by appearing to tilt towards Asia. 'The thinly veiled US threats about having Asia as an alternative to Europe are absurd', he argued. 'It's almost as if France said it no longer cared about the United States because most of our trade was with other European Community countries.' Not surprisingly, US officials had a more positive attitude towards a summit which they felt had helped clear away some of the considerable obstacles still standing in the way of a final GATT agreement.[23]

GATT

The GATT deal in December 1993 was the result of many factors, both objective, in terms of the beneficial impact the agreement would have on world trade, and subjective, in the form of Peter Sutherland (the Director General of GATT) who played a vital part in negotiations during the last six months. But an equally critical role was played by US trade representative Mickey Kantor and Sir Leon Brittan, the EU's trade commissioner. Sir Leon managed to convince the Americans that the fractious and hydra-headed EU could actually deliver an agreement, while Kantor applied sufficient pressure on the Europeans to make them move ahead. Certainly, without their combined contribution GATT might not have been signed.[24]

The GATT agreement had its winners and losers. It also involved a good degree of compromise on the American side. According to most seasoned commentators, in fact, it was Europe and not the United States that gained most from the deal. Naturally, a number of questions remained unresolved, including the contentious issue of workers' rights and labour standards. But GATT was still a great achievement for the Clinton administration and its much-criticized tough approach to trade. It was also likely to lead to a massive increase in world trade over the next ten years: between $230bn and $274bn according to one estimate, and $745bn according to the GATT Secretariat.[25] Finally, its success brought the developing nations (those which held the greatest growth potential for US companies) more completely into the traditional trading system. As Garten, a one-time sceptic about GATT, pointed out, although this meant that the new emerging markets would have 'enhanced obligations', it also implied that they would now 'have a fair shot at access to the industrialised country markets' as well. This was good news for them, for the world economy, and above all for the United States.[26]

Transforming government

The Clinton administration's support for GATT and the cause of 'open regionalism' was part of a broader strategy to establish a more dynamic global economy within which it was hoped US companies would be able to compete successfully. But they could only compete, it was argued, if they developed a more intimate relationship with government. To give meaning to this new partnership, important reforms were necessary in the way in which government itself operated. In September 1993 the 'Trade Promotion Coordinating Committee', chaired by Ron Brown of the Commerce Department, published its key study, *Toward a National Export Strategy*, which was designed to have a big impact on the way in which government functioned.[27] Viewed by the administration itself as establishing a framework 'for an unprecedented strengthening' of America's 'export promotion efforts' (and by others as a new name for old-style neo-mercantilism), the document stood at the heart of the Clinton administration's approach to international economic affairs. Though not as original as its authors claimed, it certainly impelled those working for government to think and act far more 'economically' than they had done before. Consequently, US embassy staff up to ambassadorial level were given enhanced business support. A new economics-oriented curriculum for Foreign Service Officer training was introduced. Even those working in the 'caring' foreign policy sectors, such as aid and development, were urged to calculate precisely how their work helped advance US economic interests. Indeed, the whole atmosphere in Washington changed during 1993 as government started to get more closely involved in the business of helping American business succeed.

But it was within the newly enhanced Commerce Department itself that this metamorphosis was most visible. What Brown called this 'enormous untapped potential' went through a renaissance under his leadership, effectively being transformed from an organizational backwater to an important policy player. Working on the assumption that exports not only had been, but would continue to be the most significant element in the expansion of America's GDP (having accounted for 55 per cent economic growth between 1987 and 1993 while creating more and better jobs), the Department laid out what amounted to a blueprint for improving government support for US exporters in an age of increased competition.

Briefly, the new export strategy called upon all those involved in export promotion to identify 'client groups' more effectively and focus in a more determined way on 'meeting customer needs'. In order to 'improve service' to potential customers, however, it was vital to use the resources of both the private sector and local government more effectively, and to reduce or eliminate 'government-imposed impediments to exports'. This involved quite important changes, including the elimination of most pre-existing export controls (except where these were deemed to be in the national interest). Significantly, in this area, the Commerce Department recommended a speedy liberalization of export controls on critical, normally high-value items, especially 'computers and telecommunication products'.

Taken together these changes, it was hoped, would create a more streamlined governmental machine designed for an age in which economic success or failure in world markets would determine America's future. Brown himself was in no doubt about the significance of these various reforms. Indeed, at the end of his first year in office, he thought they represented his 'proudest achievement'.[28]

Transforming research

To make America competitive it was vital not only to develop a coherent national export strategy but to implement economic reforms at home; and one of the most critical reforms contemplated by the Clinton administration (apart from deficit reduction) was in the area of federal support for research and development. Not only would a new type of partnership have to be established between the government and industrial research, but the government itself would have to rethink what sort of research it would support in a post-Cold War era. After all, what was the point of investing vast amounts of money in defence-related research (even as late as 1992 defence still consumed 60 per cent of government support for R&D) while spending on defence itself was declining as a percentage of GNP? This was seen not only as unnecessary but as an inefficient use of scarce resources that would be much better deployed enhancing the country's economic status in the world.

Clinton thus set out to change the balance in federal support between non-military and military R&D, and in 1992 announced that within six years there would be parity of esteem between the two sectors. This would involve cuts in military R&D accompanied by a gradual but measurable increase in spending on civilian R&D by 30 per cent over five years. But simply altering the balance was not enough: unless the right industries were targeted, the new partnership between the state and the private sector would lose all credibility. Thus a number of prototype projects were launched, one of the first being a $1.3bn research grant to the big three car-makers in September 1993 to develop a vehicle that would be environmentally friendly (Gore's so-called 'green car'). This was followed in the next year by other grants to industry; $1bn to develop a high performance computer and $2bn for materials research. Another $2.3bn was set aside in 1994 to encourage education in science, maths, engineering and technological subjects. The administration also announced a $1bn package in April 1994 to fund the development and manufacture of flat panel displays as used in the increasingly lucrative portable computer market. The eventual goal here was to establish four large-scale manufacturing sites in the US with a view to supplying about one-sixth of world demand.[29]

Nevertheless, a number of questions remained unanswered about this particular aspect of the administration's policy to enhance American economic power. One, clearly, was how far it would actually be able to go in reducing government spending on research for defence – a sector which had many vocal supporters in Congress. Equally, it was uncertain whether a Republican-controlled Congress would be prepared to support expensive research on non-military R&D to the degree necessary to achieve results. Finally, there were many who believed that even if Clinton could alter the whole research agenda and overcome congressional opposition, it would be quite foolish to waste money on a strategy that could never work. Thus many barriers remained to be overcome before scientific and technological research in the United States could be fully 'Clintonized'.[30]

'Big Emerging Markets'

The Clinton administration's proposed programme of gradually switching government R&D away from the military clearly could not produce quick results. It focused, therefore, on those policies which could; and one policy it pursued with great purpose was to target what it called the Big Emerging Markets, or BEMs. Ten such had been identified by the end of 1992. Significantly, five of these were in Asia-Pacific (China – including Taiwan, Hong Kong, Indonesia, India and South Korea); and three (Mexico, Brazil and Argentina) in Latin America. The others were Poland, Turkey and South Africa. Though these were not seen as alternatives to more traditional and much larger markets such as Canada, Japan or western Europe, they were all regarded as critical areas of growth into the twenty-first century. Commerce Department planners, for example, estimated that by the year 2000 US trade with these ten countries could easily exceed that with Europe and Japan combined. The CIA also stressed the importance of the BEMs, and in one report calculated that between 1994 and 2010 they would account for something like 44 per cent of non-US growth in world imports.

Having identified its target countries, the United States set out to woo the Big Emerging Markets with great determination. Revealing the same energy it had shown in Saudi Arabia in February 1994 (when after intense lobbying it had won a $6bn order for American planes) Washington seemed prepared to use all means necessary to maximize market share.[31]

One example of this more assertive US strategy was furnished by its trade activities in Brazil. Looking upon Brazil's economic potential as being huge over the longer term, the ever-active Commerce Department, under Ron Brown's guidance, consciously set out to extend its economic ties to the largest nation in Latin America. In June 1994 Brown led a high-profile American trade mission to Brazil, accompanied as usual by a large number of executives from some of the biggest US corporations. In Sao Paolo, he also opened a new $2m American commerce centre, noting in the ceremonial speech that the city had 'as many consumers as the whole of Argentina put together'. He also drew his audience's attention to the 'vital and growing importance' of US trade with Latin America as a whole. And if current trends continued, the continent, he argued, would one day overtake Europe as the main trading partner of the United States. In negotiations with the Brazilian government, Brown then deployed his not inconsiderable bargaining skills in helping the United States to win a major surveillance project (SIVAM), consisting of a mixed satellite/aircraft/radar system that would allow Brazilians to spot environmental degradation in the Amazon basin, to be more effective in drug interdiction, and that would serve other land use planning purposes.[32]

Another significant American foray was into Indonesia, like Brazil a huge and important country with a long-standing security relationship with the United States. Here both Clinton and Brown played an active part in winning orders for American firms, most notably during and just after the APEC summit in November 1994. Clinton was quite forthright and while preaching the virtues of Pacific cooperation to his neighbours, announced (without any hint of irony) that the US was engaged in cut-throat economic competition with its overseas rivals. He also emphasized that his administration, 'in contrast to previous' ones, would be 'unashamedly active in helping' American business abroad. No quarter would be expected and none given. As if to underline the seriousness of American intentions, Ron Brown (fresh from economic triumphs in Malaysia and the Philippines, where he had just acquired $650m worth of business for US companies) signed a number of contracts and memoranda with Indonesia valued at over $40bn. The biggest winner of all was the American oil giant, Exxon Corporation Exploration. As a result of US government efforts on its behalf, it signed a basic agreement valued at nearly $35bn with Indonesia's state-owned oil company, Pertamina.[33]

US successes in Indonesia were in part the result of a new credit facility offered by the Clinton administration. Involving government-to-government concessional financing linked to the purchase of donor country exports, the so-called 'Tied Aid' credit offer was specifically designed to counter foreign competition by levelling the financial playing-field for US exporters. This same facility proved equally effective in India, and within two years of Ron Brown taking over the US had signed several deals with Delhi using this particular economic vehicle.

Moreover, having identified India as one of the biggest of the new BEMs, the administration vigorously supported American firms to the tune of $300m per annum. Ron Brown also led a large US trade delegation to India in January 1995. He began his economic tour with what one observer later described as an 'inspired piece of theatre'. This involved a visit to the site of Mahatma Gandhi's cremation on the birthday of the Indian leader's most celebrated American disciple, Martin Luther King. By the time Brown flew home, it looked as if he had won at least $7bn of Indian business. Contained within this overall package was an order to supply seven out of the eight big 'fast-track' power generation projects destined to be constructed in India. It also included a deal involving the telecommunications company US West – the first privately operated corporation allowed to invest in the still backward (but potentially huge) Indian telecommunications market. More business looked likely to follow, and the Commerce Department was predicting $20bn of new American investment by the year 2000 plus a rise in US exports to $5–6bn annually – double the 1994 level.[34]

Conclusion

In its first three years the Clinton administration demonstrated a real determination to reverse what many of its more influential members saw as the nation's economic decline, to create an entirely new culture in the field of foreign policy, and to win what some of them also conceive of as the struggle for economic supremacy in the twenty-first century. To this end it pursued an extraordinarily coherent strategy which gave the lie to the argument that Clinton had, or has, no vision. But in spite of Clinton's energetic, indeed aggressive pursuit of US economic interests, there are still a number of problems with his strategy. Some have been identified by critics such as Krugman, but here I want to raise four more.

First, frenetic activity does not necessarily get rid of trade imbalances. Indeed, in spite of the continuing growth in US exports (in 1994 they expanded by over 10 per cent), the United States still continued to carry a huge trade deficit of $166bn. According to some economists this was neither particularly significant nor a reason for gloom. Nevertheless, so long as the deficit persisted, there were bound to be those calling for ever tougher action to deal with it; and that carried within it the seeds of future conflicts with other nations.

Secondly, there was within the Clinton administration an unmistakeable tendency to use the issue of competitiveness almost as a substitute for dealing with the country's own economic problems. Here one could detect a certain tension, in fact, between those who recognized that the solution to US economic ills lay at home and others who focused the greater part of their efforts on confronting and beating competitors abroad. However, because the latter could promise results, they inevitably soon become the dominant voice inside the administration. Again, this did not bode well for America's economic relations with its various competitors – the third, related problem.

Although Clinton proclaimed the virtues of multilateralism, many of the policies he pursued smacked of unfettered unilateralism. This not only contained within it the seeds of future economic conflict but had the potential for weakening the bonds holding the major democracies together. The United States after all could hardly practise dollar diplomacy one day and then expect cooperation from its allies the next.

Finally, the US obsession with competitiveness posed an even larger question about its broader mission in the world. If America's primary purpose was to win the economic race, then how could this be reconciled with its historic goal of promoting global democracy? No doubt Clinton hoped, and certainly argued, that as nations became more closely integrated into the world market, democracy would inevitably follow. This was possibly so, but only in the long term. Meanwhile, there was bound to be a very real conflict of interest: between promoting American economic objectives on the one hand and supporting the cause of human rights on the other. And one hardly needed a crystal ball to know which one the United States was most likely to sacrifice in an age of geo-economics.

Chapter 4

Planning for the next war: restructuring defence

'It may be argued that the sheer possession of vast lethal power imposes an undue strain upon mere human beings. Men are not gods, and when they gather the power of the gods in their hands they come to behave like beasts. The nation which develops inordinate military strength can hardly avoid the ultimate loss of self-restraint, the disposition to gain its ends by coercion, and the repudiation of the values of peaceful accommodation.'
– INIS L. CLAUDE, *Swords into Plowshares*[1]

The Second World War transformed the United States from a rather ordinary, inward-looking country with a limited military capacity (in 1939 its military budget stood at only $500m) into a superpower capable of shaping humanity's destiny. Certainly, without the practical experience of war waged victoriously across two oceans and three continents, the United States would not have been the force it was at the war's end. But possessing as it did by then, the atomic bomb, a spectacularly strong navy, and an enormous air force with the ability to bomb targets thousands of miles from home, it literally stood astride the globe in 1945, confident in the fact that there was no other country in the world which could seriously threaten its territorial integrity. As the first Secretary of Defense, James Forrestal, noted just two years after the war, the United States was in an almost impregnable position and would remain so as long as it could 'outproduce' everybody else, control the seas and strike against any potential foe 'with the atomic bomb'.[2]

The transition from the Second World War to the Cold War between

1945 and 1948 altered the international situation but did not in itself change America's military capabilities or bring about a militarization of its foreign policy. For insofar as the threat to Western interests was primarily political in character – as George Kennan repeatedly pointed out at the time – it was assumed that it could best be contained by economic means and the force of example. With the Berlin blockade, however, followed in rapid succession by the detonation of a Soviet atomic device, the Chinese revolution and the unexpected North Korean attack on South Korea, the United States finally felt compelled to review its grand strategy in order to confront what was now universally regarded as a serious military threat to its interests around the world.[3]

The implications of this movement from one phase of the Cold War to another were huge. First, it led the United States to develop and deploy an even greater military machine than the one it had originally inherited from the Second World War. This in time came to consist of a large and growing intercontinental strategic force, thousands of tactical nuclear weapons in Eurasia, a huge global navy, a standing army of nearly a million men, a significant and permanent military presence in western Europe, an air force capable of intercontinental bombing, and a sea and air power projection capacity that would allow the United States to move its conventional forces around the globe with relative ease. The militarization of the Cold War also changed the character and structure of the American economy. So important did military spending become, in fact, that many wondered whether the United States would ever be able to afford peace. Finally, as a result of the transition to global military containment, the United States became engaged in a dynamic arms race with the USSR. Ostensibly designed to contain Moscow's expansionary urges, its deeper purpose always was to place pressure upon the Soviet Union in the hope that one day Moscow would be impelled either to adjust to global realities or to contemplate far-reaching reform at home.[4] Indeed, according to most conservative commentators, it was the deliberate stepping-up of the arms race in the 1980s which brought the Cold War to a rapid conclusion.[5]

This chapter starts with an examination of the Bush response to the end of the Cold War and the collapse of the USSR. It then analyses Clinton's military agenda and the most important military issue facing the US in the post-Cold War era: nuclear non-proliferation. It concludes with a discussion of wider nuclear issues.

George Bush: the reluctant disarmer

In a key speech in September 1993, the then American Secretary of Defense, Les Aspin, made the interesting observation that not one, but two 'revolutions' had turned the world upside down after 1989: the first witnessed the collapse of communism in Eastern Europe; the second saw the shattering of the Soviet Union into a host of 'separate, often quarreling nations'. The former transformation brought the Cold War to an unexpected end; the latter left the United States as the sole surviving superpower in the world system.[6]

This distinction between two phases in the same process of communist decomposition is a useful way of trying to understand the rather different approaches to defence initially adopted by the Bush and the Clinton administrations. The Bush strategy, built around the concept of *Base Force* first outlined in 1990, effectively corresponded to that brief transitional era following the fall of communism in Eastern Europe when the USSR remained intact. The Clinton strategy – advanced in some detail in the so-called *Bottom Up Review* published in September 1993 – was developed after the fall of the Soviet Union.[7]

The continued existence of the Soviet Union after 1989 was at least one of the reasons why the Bush response to the fall of communism in Eastern Europe appears to have been so conservative. More than happy to claim political credit for having won the Cold War, his administration approached the new era very tentatively indeed. Certainly on defence matters it appeared to take the view that the least change was probably the best. This was apparent in the future Five Year Defense Plans (FYDPs) proposed to Congress in early 1991 and 1992. One can detect the same fear of change in the *National Security Strategy of the United States*, published just before the Soviet coup in August 1991. It was even apparent a year later after the fall of the USSR. Thus in the key *National Military Strategy of the United States*, published in January 1992, the term 'stability' appeared no less than twenty times; while in the later *National Security Strategy* stability was once again defined as America's number one security objective.[8]

Bush's refusal to 'take chances on untested situations' was also evident in his first defence budget. Though he called for a 25 per cent reduction in army personnel, military spending overall was scheduled to drop by only 10 per cent in real terms. He also refused to kill off any of the major weapons programmes developed during the high-spending Reagan years. Indeed, his early programme allowed for sizeable increases in anti-missile defence, the procurement of new strategic weapons systems and the purchase of new conventional weapons, as well as sizeable spending on research and development. Despite pressures to cut more deeply, Bush made only a few concessions to his critics. Thus although his 1991 budget specified further reductions in conventional arms, spending for fiscal year 1991 (which specifically excluded all present and future expenditures for the Persian Gulf operation) still stood 10 per cent higher than it had done twenty years previously.

Finally the Bush administration's conservatism on security issues manifested itself in its approach to nuclear arms control. Hence although the INF Treaty eliminating US and Soviet intermediate- and shorter-range missiles had been signed by Reagan and Gorbachev in December 1987 (the first ratified nuclear arms control agreement in over fifteen years), there seemed to be little urgency within the White House to push ahead with the more important and significant START deal covering strategic systems. Moreover, when START I was finally signed in the summer of 1991, it was really quite limited in scope; and at the time of its proposed full implementation by 1999, both sides would together still possess well over 15,000 nuclear warheads – twice what they had possessed at the time of the signing of SALT I back in 1972, and about the same number as existed at the time of the unsigned SALT II agreement in 1979. This hardly amounted to serious disarmament.[9]

Bush's less than enthusiastic desire to respond in a bold way to the ending of the Cold War provoked much comment; none more scathing than by Leslie Gelb of the Council on Foreign Relations. 'We face no military threats,' he wrote in April 1992. 'The Soviet Union lies in ruins.' No other state, 'Germany, Japan, Iran or a resurgent Russia, name your nightmare, can marshal military power to threaten the U.S. for perhaps a generation.' Furthermore, the United States dominated the world in a way it had never done before. Yet still it committed itself to spending 'nearly $1.5 trillion over the next five years' on defence. It made no sense, he concluded, other than as a very expensive job creation scheme for 'smart Pentagon planners', or for politicians unwilling 'to tear a million-plus workers from the Pentagon teat, toss them into the ranks of the unemployed and commit political suicide'. Much more needed to be done.[10]

Bush under pressure

At least three factors finally pushed the Bush administration towards adopting a more 'radical' approach to defence matters: the fall of the

USSR, the Gulf war, and continuing budgetary pressures upon American defence expenditure.

The collapse of the Soviet Union

In spite of the many changes which had taken place in the world since 1989, the USSR, according to the official US line, remained a heavily armed 'superpower' with formidable 'military capabilities'. As Dick Cheney noted in the ninth edition of *Soviet Military Power*, published almost a year after the fall of the Berlin Wall, 'prudence' demanded that the United States continued to focus on this, 'the most dangerous challenge' to US national security. It was true that the intentions of the Soviet regime had undergone a significant (though not necessarily permanent) change because of Gorbachev. But 'intentions', he argued in classic Cold War terms, were 'not enough to support dramatic changes in our own level of preparedness'. For this to happen, it was first necessary to 'see fundamental and enduring changes in both the capabilities and character of Soviet military power'.[11] Then and only then would the US be able to contemplate more far-reaching reforms.[12]

The Gulf war

If the collapse of the USSR permitted the US to contemplate greater reductions in its military arsenal (in January 1993, for instance, Bush and Yeltsin signed START II reducing US and Russian strategic offensive arms by eliminating all MIRVed ICBMs), the Gulf war impelled it to rethink the balance between its traditional Cold War commitment to western Europe and its military role in other parts of the world. For political reasons the United States would continue to base a proportion of its forces on the European continent, though at a much lower level than envisaged in the Treaty on Conventional Forces in Europe (CFE) signed in November 1990. But it was self-evident that in the new era the real challenge to American power was going to come in unstable regions such as the Middle East and the Korean peninsula.

This shift of emphasis, with all its implications for military doctrine and US force levels, began to impact on the security debate during late 1990 and early 1991. The discussion continued during 1992, and the transition towards a new regional focus was more or less completed with the publication of Bush's last defence review, the *National Security Strategy*, in January 1993. This document openly accepted that US interests were increasingly likely to be challenged not by Russia, but from 'regional instabilities'. These were now the principal danger to global order.[13]

Budgetary pressures

Finally, in planning for national security, the Bush administration could not escape from economic realities. It thus found itself under growing congressional pressure to reduce defence spending as at least one way of controlling the budget deficit. There was nothing new in this. In fact, in real terms, military expenditure had been falling since the second half of the 1980s as a result of the Gramm-Rudman-Hollings Bill of 1986.[14] However, with the passing of the Cold War, the way was now open for even deeper cuts, according to an increasingly cost-conscious Congress. The result of the ensuing series of battles between the two branches of government was a suggestion by the White House, in its budget for 1992, of a 21.7 per cent cut in money spent on defence, spread over five years. Though this went much further than anything ever proposed before, Congress was still not satisfied and urged even greater savings.

Clinton and defence

The election of a president who promised that he would not only focus 'laser-like' on the material concerns of ordinary citizens, but bring military spending down as part of a wider programme to reinvigorate the American economy, was bound to have a significant impact on the US defence debate. In fact, according to Clinton, such a debate had not yet taken place. The previous administration, he argued, had simply responded in an *ad hoc* fashion to a rapidly evolving situation. What was needed was a completely new approach that looked at security policy from the 'bottom up'. Believing that Bush had only implemented a slightly less expensive version of traditional policies (a 'downsized force largely shaped by Cold War priorities', as Les Aspin put it) Clinton promised an entirely new look – a coherent long-term plan based on a clearer definition of threats, a more precise analysis of the type of forces necessary to meet these threats, and a more reasonable assessment of the outlays that would be required to pay for US national security needs in a post-Soviet era.

The Bottom Up Review

The Clinton defence strategy, as outlined in the *Bottom Up Review*, was released on 1 September 1993. Though organized around what Aspin claimed was an original 'threat-based' approach to military planning, in fact it contained little with which Bush would have disagreed.

Significantly, the first danger identified in the *Review* was posed by what it termed 'large-scale aggression by major regional powers with interests antithetical to our own'. Such aggression did not necessarily threaten the direct existence of the United States. On the other hand, if it was not dealt with in a decisive manner (and here the lessons of the Gulf war loomed large) it could present a very real challenge to America's control over vital economic resources, to the balance in power in some parts of the world, as well as to US credibility. The *Review* pinpointed two such regions where aggression was most likely to arise: the Middle East and the Korean peninsula. While noting that this should not be taken as a 'prediction of future conflicts', it was fairly clear in its assessment that these were the areas where serious challenges to world order by 'well-armed regional powers' would be most likely to arise in the future.

The second 'new' danger facing the United States was associated with the proliferation of nuclear, biological and chemical weapons in general, and in particular of those large stocks of weapons remaining in the former Soviet Union. Potentially this was the greatest threat facing the world in the modern era. The *Review* saw a close connection between the danger of regional aggression and the problem of proliferation; for those same regional powers which threatened the peace were especially keen to acquire nuclear weapons. Moreover, if they gained access to such weapons, they would be able to challenge the United States more successfully. Here again the shadow of the Gulf war hung heavily over US military deliberations. As Aspin had pointed out in an earlier discussion of the issue, if Saddam had had nuclear weapons prior to the invasion of Kuwait he might not have won the war but he might have been able to intimidate the US or its allies into making dangerous concessions. Keeping nuclear weapons out of hands like his was therefore critical.[15]

Finally, the *Review* identified a less immediate, but equally important long-term danger to US interests: the threat of democratic reversal in the former USSR. On this it was difficult to be specific, for the danger of dictatorships had not yet emerged. But if it did this would inevitably mean 'a less peaceful and more difficult world for the United States'. It would also create major problems for Clinton. For although the point was not made explicitly (it went without saying), a new Cold War with a less friendly, more authoritarian Russia would compromise his domestic agenda which in large part depended on getting military spending down and thereafter keeping it low.

From this specification of new dangers, the *Bottom Up Review* outlined the force structure needed to guarantee American security into the twenty-first century. Given its strong regional focus, the prime emphasis, not surprisingly, was on smaller, more versatile and mobile forces that could be sent quickly overseas. Power projection, heavy lift and logistical support were thus central when it came to fighting the wars of the future. But how many wars? On this there had been a good deal of debate. The important and controversial conclusion arrived at was that the United States should be able not just to win one war (while holding the line somewhere else), but to win two wars more or less simultaneously. This 'win-win' option, as it became known, was adopted for at least three reasons. One was economic, insofar as the Department of Defense claimed that it was relatively inexpensive to move from 'win-hold-win' to 'win-win'. It was also hoped to avoid a situation in which the United States would make simultaneous wars more likely by planning for anything less. Finally, by fielding numbers sufficient to win two wars 'nearly simultaneously', it was assumed this would provide a hedge against the possibility of any future adversary confronting the United States with a larger than expected force. In other words, by planning for the worst, the worst might be avoided.[16]

But what would all this cost? On this there was a great deal of confusion and acrimonious debate. Given his own priorities Clinton obviously looked forward to large savings. Hence, if all went according to plan, outlays on national defence would fall by an average of 4.5 per cent per annum between 1994 and 1999: in real terms a drop of nearly 25 per cent. This would bring military spending down to just over 3 per cent of GNP by the turn of the century, the lowest ratio for the entire postwar period. But the cuts envisaged by Clinton were not that much deeper than those already planned by Bush. Bush's last defence budget over five years would have cost the nation $1,325bn; Clinton's about $1,221bn – a difference of only $104bn. Hardly staggering in a country where the annual budget was well over a trillion dollars.[17]

Critiques of the Review

The Clinton review on defence was classically centrist in character. For this reason it was attacked by both liberals who felt it did not go far enough, and conservatives who thought that it went much too far. Hostile to Clinton on nearly everything else, the right could barely contain its contempt. Colin Gray, for one, could find nothing positive to say about the *Bottom Up Review*. In his view it was not informed by a clear definition of what actually constituted the American national interest in the post-Soviet world; it was driven less by a clear notion of the threats facing the United States than by a desire to justify already agreed reductions in the defence budget; and it was militarily flawed as well. In fact, in Gray's opinion, there was actually no way of knowing whether the force structure advocated by Clinton would even be able to wage and win the two near-simultaneous regional conflicts specified in the *Bottom Up Review*.[18]

Another conservative critic (a defence consultant in the second Reagan administration) was even more scathing, arguing that the Clinton approach was utterly disastrous because it was shaped almost entirely by the President's 'determination to carry out budgetary cuts twice as large as those promised during the [election] campaign'. The result, he concluded, was a security fiasco in which US forces would be called upon to do things that were impossible given the resources at their disposal. The President faced a stark and simple choice therefore: either to maintain the budget or abandon the pretence that the win-win strategy was an option.[19]

Others were less vituperative but came to similar conclusions. Many, for example, agreed there was a basic mismatch between the force requirements needed to fight two wars and the means available to pay for them.[20] According to one analyst the *Review* also appeared to offer no guidance for 'when force should be used, what interests should be defended, and why two major regional conflicts should form the basis for planning'.[21] Another critic even wondered whether the US military was falling into the trap of most successful military organizations: that of preparing to fight the last war (in this case the Gulf war) instead of planning for the next one.[22]

But not all the attacks came from conservative or mainstream sources. Others, of a more liberal persuasion, were equally critical, on the grounds that Clinton was devoting not too few, but far too many resources to national security. As they pointed out, even after all the proposed cuts had been implemented, the United States would still be spending nearly as much on defence as the rest of the world put together. Moreover, though Clinton claimed he was breaking with tradition and doing something rather radical, in many ways he was only paring down defence rather than transforming it. Finally, they believed the *Bottom Up Review* seriously overstated the regional threats to international security. For instance, none of the potential adversaries it identified actually possessed a modern industrial base or up-to-date military equipment. Nor did they pose a direct threat to the American people or to America's core industrial or trading partners. In short the *Review* was looking for demons where none actually existed.[23]

Countering nuclear proliferation

Three months after the *Bottom Up Review* was published, Secretary of Defense Les Aspin announced what he called the 'Defense Counter-proliferation Initiative' to deal directly with the 'new danger' facing the world from a 'handful of nuclear devices' controlled by 'rogue states' and even 'terrorist groups'. Some assumed that this was much less of a problem than the Soviet nuclear arsenal. Not so, according to Aspin. In fact, precisely because these states and groups were less easily deterred and far more unpredictable in their behaviour than the USSR, they constituted as much if not more of a danger to the international order.

Aspin did not precisely define 'counterproliferation' in his December 1993 statement. However, a National Security Council memorandum in February 1994 offered the following clarification: 'proliferation' was the spread of nuclear, biological or chemical weapons – hence 'nonproliferation' was characterized as the attempt to prevent this or reverse it, normally by diplomatic means; 'counterproliferation', on the other hand, was defined as using the full range of political, economic and military tools to combat proliferation. It thus implied a far more interventionist (some feared more aggressive) approach by the United States. But this was deemed to be necessary by US policy-makers in the new international environment.[24]

Effective measures aimed at countering the threat of proliferation had to do more than just punish potential proliferators, however; they also needed to focus on what motivated states to acquire or sell dangerous weapons in the first place. In this sense, US policy aimed to attack the root causes of proliferation as much as impose sanctions on those who threatened to acquire or keep weapons of mass destruction. It tried to do this in at least two ways. The first was through the provision of security guarantees – this was crucial, for example, to the willingness of Ukraine, Belarus and Kazakhstan to abandon nuclear weapons. The second tool was the extension of assistance to those ready to observe non-proliferation norms. Ukraine, for instance, received nuclear rods from Moscow for power generation as compensation for nuclear weapons sent back to Russia. The Korean Energy Development Organization (KEDO) also promised critical help to North Korea to replace power lost by the termination of its nuclear programme.

In the struggle to deal with the problem of proliferation, the United States had to address what many saw as the key to the whole question: Russia and the states of the former Soviet Union. As Chapter 5 describes, the problems here were immense, ranging from the multiplication of weapons states within the former USSR itself, to the diversion of former Soviet nuclear scientists to other countries, through to the theft and smuggling of nuclear material. To deal with all these eventualities the US undertook a number of measures. These started under Bush when in 1991 Congress authorized the use of $400m of defence funds for assistance to Russia and other newly independent states to dismantle nuclear weapons. By FY1995 $1.6bn had been used for this specific purpose. On 23 June 1994, Vice-President Al Gore and Russian Prime Minister Viktor Chernomyrdin also signed agreements to shut down plutonium reactors in Russia and to cease the production of plutonium for military purposes. In November 1994, the Clinton administration even made public a secret mission to Kazakhstan to retrieve 600 kg of bomb-grade uranium from a poorly guarded facility. There were also unconfirmed reports of US intelligence monitoring the movement of material and scientists from the former USSR to nations (hostile or otherwise) in the Third World.

Assessing the effectiveness of these various countermeasures was by no means easy. Clearly there were important achievements: Ukraine became a party to the Nuclear Non-Proliferation Treaty; North Korea agreed to a framework for dismantling its nuclear programme; and China accepted a global ban on the export of all ground-to-ground missiles with capabilities controlled by the Missile Technology Control Regime (MTCR). Yet it would be foolish to underestimate the scale of the problem. Some experts, in fact, believed that the situation was almost uncontrollable over the longer term – in effect that proliferation was inevitable – and that the United States should plan for the worst, either by pushing ahead with a limited missile defence system of its own, or by withdrawing from its defence commitments around the world. Some even argued that the United States should openly accept proliferation by friendly, more moderate states and deal only with the arms acquired by unfriendly, aggressive states. However, this view was never likely to be adopted as official policy: it would go against the USA's stated goal of limiting the number of nuclear powers in the world, and the distinction between friendly and unfriendly proliferators would be almost impossible to maintain over the longer term. Most US policy-makers felt it would be both unwise and unnecessary to abandon policies which had not only proved relatively effective, but which still remained in the US national interest.[25]

The Non-Proliferation Treaty, 1995

Absolutely critical to the maintenance of the non-proliferation regime was the indefinite extension of the Non-Proliferation Treaty (NPT) in the spring of 1995. The NPT represented the cornerstone of the non-proliferation regime. Hence its demise, or even the possibility that it would not be indefinitely extended, would have spelt disaster for US policies. It would have been fatal for the International Atomic Energy Agency (IAEA) and its safeguard systems. It would also have led to the unravelling of multilateral export controls. Finally, its collapse might even have undermined the norm of non-use of nuclear weapons which had prevailed since the end of the Second World War. From the American perspective, therefore, a great deal was at stake.[26]

But in the lead-up to the crucial meeting in New York it was by no means certain that the NPT would be ratified. A number of Third World countries, in particular, threatened to vote against indefinite extension. Their arguments were not without some moral or intellectual substance. The nuclear 'haves', they pointed out, had not lived by their original promise contained in Article 6 of the 1970 NPT to undertake 'general and complete disarmament under strict and effective international control'. Thus the NPT had failed in one of its primary tasks. There was also deep concern that at least three countries in good international standing (including Israel) had crossed the nuclear threshold without the United States doing a great deal about it – an argument that carried a good deal of force in the Arab world. It was pointed out, moreover, that at the heart of the NPT there was a profound hypocrisy which permitted certain powers – invariably large ones – to possess nuclear weapons but denied this privilege to others.

Given the importance of the NPT on the one hand and the uncertainty about its final passage on the other, the Clinton administration went into political overdrive to persuade the nuclear have-nots to support it. This involved much creative arm-twisting, to the frustration of many diplomats from developing countries who opposed indefinite extension. One Latin American diplomat even went so far as to admit later that if all the countries attending the NPT conference had had 'the opportunity to express their views freely the indefinite extension would never have won'. Certainly, considerable pressure appears to have been applied to Mexico. Gore also delivered a firm message to the Arab states (particularly Egypt) in March 1995 that Washington not only wanted, but expected them to back indefinite extension of the NPT despite Israel's refusal to sign the accord.[27]

In the end the NPT was made permanent, though without a formal vote. A declaration of principles spelling out the need for nuclear disarmament, as well as for a stronger review process to check on disarmament efforts, was adopted. An eleventh-hour hitch was overcome when a resolution singling out Israel for special mention was watered down. Objections by Iran also meant that the eventual approval of the Treaty was not described as being by consensus. Instead the NPT was renewed by general acclamation.

The successful passage of the NPT was obviously welcomed in Washington. Yet as Hans Blix, the head of the International Atomic Agency, noted, even though the NPT had been extended, the nuclear powers had a lot to do to keep their side of the deal. At the very least they would have to agree to a complete test ban. More critically, perhaps, they would also have to pay more than just lip service to the principle of disarmament. In spite of the decision, therefore, the future still remained uncertain. As Zachary Davis has observed, the indefinite extension of the NPT did not represent the 'endgame' for non-proliferation, or even a solution, but part of an ongoing effort to hold the line on the spread of nuclear weapons. The struggle would have to go on.[28]

Rethinking nuclear weapons?

Although the *Bottom Up Review* did not deal directly with nuclear weapons, it did promise to look at US nuclear weapons strategy in depth. This review, it was argued, would tackle several problems simultaneously including the list of targets in the former USSR, the size of the nuclear arsenal, how it was to be deployed by land, sea and air, and the way it was to be used either to deter or punish old or new enemies. What it did not promise, however, was a revolution. There was no hint, for instance, that the United States would be adopting the policy of 'no first use'. And for the present the Clinton administration was not looking much beyond START II. Les Aspin in fact went out of his way to dampen down unwarranted expectations. As he made clear at the press conference announcing the review, the Cold War was over and the Soviet Union was no more, but the post-Cold War world would decidedly not be post-nuclear.[29]

The *Nuclear Posture Review* (finally published in September 1994) was thus bound to be disappointing for those who felt the time had come for an even fuller denuclearization of the American arsenal and of American thinking about the role of nuclear weapons. The headline in the *Washington Post* the day after its appearance said it all: 'Clinton decides to retain Bush nuclear arms policy'.[30] Admittedly the nuclear review provided a thorough discussion of many aspects of nuclear policy including doctrine, force structure, operations, safety and security and arms control. But it came nowhere near doing what Aspin's successor Bill Perry said it might do, which was to change the way the United States thought about nuclear weapons. Even the justification for retaining nuclear weapons was a traditional one, based as it was upon a rather gloomy or unpredictable reading of developments in the former USSR.

The somewhat conventional nature of the nuclear review should not of course obscure the fact that much had changed since the fall of communism. As Aspin noted, by the mid-1990s the US nuclear stockpile had been reduced by nearly 60 per cent, while spending on strategic forces had fallen from $47bn in 1984 (or 13.6 per cent of the defence budget) to $12.4bn (5 per cent of the budget).[31] But there was no hiding the fact that the *Nuclear Posture Review* was something of a damp squib. This is presumably why it provoked hardly any debate at all on the conservative right. The real attack, in fact, came from other quarters. Indeed, according to its more liberal critics, even after the full implementation of START I and II, the United States and the former Soviet Union together would still have 3,500 nuclear warheads aimed at each other. This seemed an absurdly high number for two countries seeking to build a new strategic alliance. The *Nuclear Posture Review* was also regarded as disappointing because it failed to ask fundamental questions about the role of nuclear weapons in general and the logic of deterrence in particular.

Finally, in the eyes of its critics, there was a contradiction in the US position between maintaining a substantial nuclear arsenal and trying to uphold a nuclear non-proliferation regime premised on an assumption of disarmament. There were many, in fact, who believed that the US would not be able to prevent the horizontal spread of nuclear weapons (i.e. to those countries that had not previously possessed them) unless it did more about its own nuclear arsenal. As one of the sharper brains on the Washington political scene observed, the post-Cold War era presented the United States with a paradox: a less problematic military relationship with Russia, but a more dangerous situation in terms of nuclear proliferation. The only way of dealing with this, he argued, was by striking a new nuclear bargain in which the 'haves' (notably the United States) would reduce their arsenals towards zero in exchange for the 'have nots' accepting tougher verification and enforcement measures. Unfortunately, the nuclear review had not even hinted at this and had therefore weakened the non-proliferation regime from which all, including the US, were supposed to benefit.[32]

Conclusion

Four factors have shaped the American defence debate since 1989: the collapse of Soviet power in Eastern Europe, the fall of the USSR, the Gulf war, and budgetary constraints. Individually any one of these variables would have had an enormous impact on US defence. Taken together however they have produced something of a minor revolution. Many of course insist the United States has been too timid, while others feel it has been too bold in its response to the new situation. But given its interests, its evident desire to remain a world power, and the uncertainties still present in the international system, the United States could probably not have acted differently.

But what of the future? There are three points worth mentioning. First, despite the fact that the United States will remain in a stronger military position than at any time since the end of the Second World War, theoretically with the capacity to do more or less anything it chooses, there are enormous constraints upon what it can do in practice – the most obvious one being the American people themselves who, in the absence of a clear and present danger, seem increasingly unwilling to support the use of military power abroad. Even mobilizing consent for the war against Iraq in 1991 took an enormous amount of time and political patience, and it is extremely unlikely that the US will be faced in the future with such an easy target or obvious threat as Saddam Hussein.

Secondly, under conditions where the whole focus of foreign policy is shifting, the pressure to reduce what many see as wasteful military spending is bound to continue. Certainly there are factors militating against this, including the desire to protect the US industrial defence base, and demands from a new generation of conservative Republicans to increase Pentagon spending. But these will not be able to counter the almost irresistible economic logic impelling the defence budget downwards as a percentage of GNP.

Finally, as military spending does come down, this will have a significant and not always positive impact on the US economy. One of the big problems facing the United States will be to find a suitable alternative to national security (if indeed there is one) as a means of generating economic activity. Certainly as military spending declines a high price is going to be paid; in many ways it has already been paid in terms of large lay-offs in defence industries, reduced funding for scientific research, and declining opportunities for the less advantaged (especially African Americans) who previously used the military as their stepping stone to a better way of life. Adjusting to post-Cold War realities could be a much more painful process than opponents of the military-industrial complex ever thought likely.[33]

Chapter 5

Strategic alliance or cold peace? Managing post-Communist Russia

'It is overwhelmingly in Russia's own interest,
as well as ours, that the forces advocating
and aspiring to integration prevail over
other forces that are also much in evidence –
those of extremist nationalism, xenophobia,
and neo-imperialism.'
– STROBE TALBOTT[1]

Between 1945 and 1991 three attempts were made by the United States to construct some sort of partnership with the Soviet Union. The first such attempt was undertaken by F.D. Roosevelt. Believing that it was now possible to persuade a war-weary, post-revolutionary (but increasingly influential) Soviet regime to play by the rules of the international game, Roosevelt sought to draw the USSR back into the fold in an attempt to build his own liberal version of a new world order. His grand strategy quickly collapsed, however, and within two years of his death his much-criticized and much-misunderstood project was increasingly regarded by US policy-makers as a foolhardy venture that had led to the inevitable appeasement of Soviet communism.

This in part explains why the next serious effort at bridge-building was not undertaken for over a quarter of a century. But after 1968, Richard Nixon, faced with a profound crisis of American power, felt impelled to find a way in which the United States could maintain its own dominance in a post-Vietnam era of nuclear parity with the USSR. He chose to do this by using the division between China and the Soviet Union, the promise of arms control, and the offer of trade expansion to draw Moscow in from the cold. Nevertheless, after a positive beginning, superpower detente quickly ran into trouble and by early 1975 had more or less completely collapsed.

The third and most serious attempt to establish an American–Soviet partnership was made by George Bush after 1989. With Eastern Europe now liberated and the USSR rapidly retreating from the Third World, Bush clearly hoped to succeed where Roosevelt had failed in using the instrument of the United Nations (now operating as was originally intended) to build a stable world order in association with the Soviet Union. This new deal, in which the Soviet Union was cast in the role of junior partner, obviously held many attractions for an America seeking to reduce the burden of world leadership in the post-Cold War era. But once more the strategy of incorporation imploded: not because of deep systemic divisions between the two countries or US fears about a rising Soviet threat, but rather because of the collapse of the USSR. This event, with its extraordinary potential for causing chaos and disorder, impelled US policy-makers to think once again about one of 'the greatest challenges' confronting the United States in the last decade of the twentieth century.[2]

This chapter looks at American efforts to deal with this challenge. The first part examines the impact of the 'Russian question' upon the presidential contest of 1992. This is followed by an analysis of Clinton's attempt to build what he called a 'strategic' partnership with post-Soviet reform, and a discussion of the contradictions in that policy and the possible alternatives to it. Finally, I will argue that although Clinton is unlikely to abandon Russia (even after Russia's crude attempt to crush the rebels in Chechenia), there is little hope of his actually building a genuine alliance with Russian reform. This will not lead to a new Cold War or even perhaps a 'cold peace'. But there are strong reasons for believing that the relationship between the United States and Russia will remain a difficult one, primarily because the reform process in Russia itself has turned out to be far more complex than Clinton had earlier assumed.

The 'Russian question' and the 1992 election

Although the 1992 presidential election was the first in the postwar period in which the Cold War played no role, the issue of what to do about Russia did figure in the debates which finally led to Clinton's victory.

According to Clinton, Bush had failed in at least three ways in his policy towards the former Soviet Union. The first was in his misjudged loyalty to Gorbachev and his failure to support Yeltsin early enough. The conclusions the US electorate was supposed to draw from this were fairly clear: that Clinton was far better placed to deal with Yeltsin than Bush; and that Bush had betrayed core American values by favouring an unelected President of the former Soviet Union over and above the elected President of Russia.

The accusation that Bush preferred Gorbachev to Yeltsin was related in turn to the complaint that the Republican administration had been more concerned with preserving the integrity of the USSR than in supporting the cause of self-determination. What this had led to, in effect, was President Bush 'aligning the United States with Mikhail Gorbachev's efforts to prop up the stagnant and despised Soviet centre, long after it was apparent that hopes for democratic reform had shifted to Boris Yeltsin and the republics'.[3] Clinton's main adviser on Russian affairs, Strobe Talbott, made much the same point in an influential piece published in *Foreign Affairs*. Bush, he argued, had been much too enthusiastic in his 'support for President Gorbachev's attempt to preserve the essential structure of the Soviet Union'. This was triply unfortunate, he believed. It implied the United States was more sensitive to Soviet needs than it was to the aspirations of those seeking to escape from the Soviet yoke. Moreover as a policy it failed to recognize that the USSR was doomed. It also represented a betrayal of American principles.[4]

Clinton's third, and perhaps most telling criticism of the Bush policy revolved around the controversial issue of aid. Adopting the line made popular by former president Richard Nixon during the 1992 election campaign, Clinton insisted that Bush had lacked imagination when it came to dealing with Russian reform – being more inclined to follow the cautious advice of bankers than to look at the problem from a geopolitical standpoint. A new Marshall Plan may have been out of the question.[5] But it was still important to give the former USSR much more material support: partly because it was in America's long-term economic interest to do so but, more critically, because if the United States remained an economic spectator, there was every chance that having won the Cold War it would now lose the peace. And this, he concluded, would represent not only a historic tragedy, but a political disaster as well.[6]

Towards a 'Strategic Alliance' with Russian reform

The success or failure of Russian reform was thus a first order concern for the United States.[7] But merely recognizing the need for change was not enough. The US now had to go beyond that and build what President

Clinton came to characterize as a 'strategic alliance' or a 'new democratic partnership' with Russian reform. There were, in his opinion, at least five connected reasons for doing so.[8]

The first had to do with the reform process itself. The United States might not be able to play a 'decisive' part in the great Russian drama. On the other hand, if Washington remained what Clinton called a 'bystander', reform could easily fail. The US would thus have to be far more proactive – for example by persuading major lending institutions to be more sympathetic to Russia's needs. It could also try much harder to promote inward American investment. There were other measures it could take as well, such as encouraging privatization, offering advice and training Russian managers, which might help lay the foundation for market success over the long term.[9]

A second reason for becoming more seriously engaged was to help manage the potentially explosive transition from empire to self-determining nations in the former USSR.[10] The end of the Soviet empire had opened up a Pandora's box of problems, and devising a coherent strategy to deal with these was a priority. This was no easy job. However, the Clinton administration (like its predecessor) could not wash its hands of the situation, and through a combination of economic inducement, political mediation and reassurance (both to Russia and to the other republics) it tried to encourage the development of what Warren Christopher hoped would one day become 'strong bilateral relations' between the 'new independent states'.[11] If this was successful it would make a major contribution to international stability. If it was not, the US might be facing another Yugoslavia, with nuclear weapons thrown in for good measure.

This was the third reason for continued engagement with Russia. START II obviously represented a major milestone in the history of arms control. But even when it was implemented (and there was a chance that it might not be) Russia would still possess a significant nuclear capability. Moreover, it was imperative to prevent, or control, the spread of nuclear weapons following the break-up of the Soviet Union.[12] This goal (one official defined 'non-proliferation' as '*the* arms control priority of the post-Cold War world')[13] impelled the Clinton administration to develop close ties to Russia and the other republics: partly because the fall of the USSR threatened the 'reliability of Moscow's centralized command and control' over nuclear systems; partly because near-bankrupt nations such as Russia and Ukraine might try to sell nuclear 'equipment and material in the international marketplace'; and partly because there were tens of thousands of poor or unemployed nuclear scientists and engineers in the former Soviet Union who might be tempted to sell their services abroad.[14]

A fourth and equally important reason for establishing ever stronger links with Russia was related to the wider issue of world order and America's place within it. Obviously, by the time Clinton entered the White House, the traditional Soviet threat had evaporated. But Russia – by virtue of its size, geographic location, continuing membership of the nuclear club, position on the UN Security Council and still significant diplomatic resources – remained a force in international relations which no US president could afford to ignore. If it had not been for Russia, after all, the Gulf conflict might not have been brought to a successful conclusion, and there would have been no possibility of a settlement in South Africa or the Middle East either. Russia simply could not be ignored. Moreover, its ability to influence world events made it a particularly attractive partner for a president who had a strong desire to reduce America's overseas commitments and share the burden of world management with other friendly powers. Indeed, in Clinton's version of the new world order, in which the United States was neither willing nor able to act as the 'world cop', a secure and integrated Russia had several important parts to play: as a barrier to the potential ambitions of (usually unspecified) nations in the Eurasian 'heartland'; as a secular dam to the spread of Islamic fundamentalism; and finally as a general stabilizer in a still uncertain world in which the United States was seeking to reduce costs.

Finally, the administration sought a deal with Moscow not just for global reasons but for domestic purposes as well. In fact, according to one seasoned commentator, the success or failure of the Clinton presidency depended in large part upon events in Russia. Clinton indeed feared that any increase in tensions would play into the hands of his conservative opponents at home. A new 'cold peace', moreover, would make it more difficult for him to realize his economic goal of reducing military spending. He was also sensitive to the fact that without a quiescent international scene, he would be unable to focus his attention on the economy. If that attention drifted, or more importantly was impelled to shift by a major international crisis caused by events in Russia, then his whole domestic programme would be put in jeopardy.[15]

The contradictions of Clinton

Building a partnership with Moscow was thus a necessity for Clinton, and in his first months in office he played his 'Russian card' with great care and skill. In the process he also revealed that when necessary he was more than capable of setting a clear agenda on a major international issue: even his political opponents had to concede that on this question he was both decisive and convincing.[16] Nevertheless, his apparently coherent strategy contained a number of inherent contradictions that were obscured initially by the President's clarity of vision, the sheer enthusiasm with which he presented his case, and the strong support he seemed to be receiving at home for his policy.

First, in spite of Clinton's bold appeal for more American and Western support for Russia, little new money was in fact forthcoming. He did manage to wring a few economic concessions from his allies and the International Monetary Fund. For example, the West was persuaded to reschedule Russia's foreign debt and the IMF to reduce the conditions Russia had to meet in order to be eligible for Fund loans. Yet these concessions were hardly revolutionary, and were certainly not enough to kick-start a failing Russian economy.

Perhaps Clinton should not be blamed personally for not being able to deliver on his earlier economic promises. In many ways he was trapped by forces outside his control: fiscal problems at home, the failure of the Russians themselves to implement meaningful economic reforms, and the orthodoxy of the wider financial community which looked askance at the idea of sinking money into the former USSR. However, when he failed to translate his fine words into concrete economic results, he not only weakened his own credibility but left his putative Russian allies in a most exposed position – ridiculed on the one hand for not getting the support they had apparently been promised, and attacked on the other for being mere puppets of the United States.[17]

The second problem with the Clinton strategy was less economic than political. Although his administration spoke of its support for post-Soviet reform in general, in reality the main thrust of American policy was directed towards Russia. Naturally, US officials tried to reassure the other republics, arguing that backing for Russia did not imply indifference to, or neglect of, the others. Christopher even reassured them that the US was totally committed to their independence and would 'assist in their integration into the world community'. Yet there was little disguising the fact that in its essentials, US policy was taken to mean a 'Russia first' policy. This had a number of negative consequences, the most important being that it fuelled non-Russian suspicion of American motives. In fact, many could see little difference in practice between Bush's earlier position on the USSR and Clinton's position on Russia.

A third dilemma for Clinton was that his strategy was premised on the assumption that there was at least a coincidence, and possibly an identity, of interest between Russia and the United States on larger international issues. By the beginning of 1993, however, this simply could not be taken for granted. The brief era of 'Mr Yes', as Sergei Karaganov characterized Russian foreign policy after autumn 1991, was drawing to a close. As Andrei Kozyrev observed in late 1992, Russia had interests of its own which did not necessarily coincide with those of America. Yeltsin apparently agreed. Indeed, he chastised the United States a month later for having displayed a certain 'tendency to dictate its own terms' on international questions, adding for good measure that from now on Russia would no longer be as compliant as it had been before.[18]

Clinton could have responded to this new assertiveness with a series of tough measures, but if he had done so his wider strategy would have been compromised. He thus chose the lesser of two evils, which meant trying to manage the new Russian challenge rather than confronting it directly. This was not without merit as a policy, especially in the 'near abroad' where the US had little real influence, even less inclination to be drawn in itself, and few major interests either. Here, therefore, it attempted to get the Russians to agree to an international code of practice which drew a line between those 'interventions' which were legitimate – separating warring factions, protecting Russian nationals, or guaranteeing regional stability – and others that were not, such as the use of proxies merely to extend Moscow's influence.[19] In theory this may have sounded fine. In practice, however, this distinction proved much more difficult to draw; and in the end, the only result was to leave Clinton open to the damaging charge of providing a cover for and turning a blind eye to Russian imperialism.[20]

The fourth problem facing Clinton revolved around the issue of NATO expansion. His administration assumed there was no inherent contradiction between its desire to engage with Russia and its wish to reassure the East Europeans that they had some sort of future within NATO. The United States, it insisted, could both build a partnership with Moscow and draw the East Europeans into the close relationship they all seemed to be demanding. But Russia was clearly opposed to any move that involved NATO expansion towards its frontiers, arguing that the Alliance was still US-dominated and that Russia would never be given a 'full voice' within it. Most Russians believed (rightly or wrongly) that the main purpose of the Alliance was to contain Russia. Not surprisingly, therefore, they had no interest in seeing NATO extended.[21]

Clinton's attempt to square this particular circle was difficult enough. But his biggest problem lay not here but within Russia itself, where the situation remained extraordinarily fragile. Certainly for a president elected on the promise that he would push Russia more rapidly along the capitalist road, Clinton had little to show for his efforts twelve months after his election. Again, one could hardly blame the US for this. However, few could have predicted that things would be so difficult – least of all the ever-upbeat occupant of the White House who had staked all on a reform process in a nation that lurched from one near-fatal crisis to another. Yeltsin managed to negotiate the first of these in April 1993 when he won his referendum. He then navigated the next one, but only by confronting and finally closing down the Russian parliament in October. The third crisis, however, proved far more difficult to resolve, not merely because the December elections revealed strong opposition to economic change, but more significantly because those hostile to the market now had a genuine democratic mandate. This was a disaster of the first order that was bound to have serious consequences in the United States.

Zhirinovsky and after

Perhaps one index of the seriousness with which the Clinton administration viewed the situation in Russia was its half-hearted public attempts to play down the significance of the elections of December 1993. The official line at first, therefore, was to make light of the anti-reform vote, more or less dismissing it as a 'protest' against short-term problems that would evaporate once things improved.[22] But according to one source, the White House was 'startled and shaken' by the outcome.[23] Al Gore, it is reliably reported, was 'dazed and speechless' when the results came in.[24] Not surprisingly, confusion abounded, and was reflected in certain statements made by leading Clinton officials concerning one of the causes of the Russian crisis. While accepting that the deeper reason for Russia's problems lay within the country itself, Gore and then Talbott (in what was seen at first as a major shift in policy) attempted to place at least some of the blame on Western economic policies. In Talbott's famous phrase there had been too much imposed 'shock' and not enough 'therapy' in Russia.[25] Hence it was necessary, or so he implied, both to slow down on the reforms and to take account of their negative social consequences.

The net result of this intervention was unfortunate, to say the least. It upset the IMF and the economically more orthodox members of the

Clinton team.[26] It also gave the impression that the administration was now split between soft liberals and hard-nosed monetarists. Moreover, it undermined the position of those in Russia who had been advocating radical economic measures.[27] Talbott's comments also called forth a wave of criticism from analysts such as Jeffrey Sachs who made the obvious point that whatever the causes of Russia's problems, they had little or nothing to do with an imaginary shock therapy that had never been administered to the patient, except for a brief four-month period in 1992.[28]

Once the dust had settled the White House set about picking its way through what looked like the debris of a failed policy. Some modifications would clearly have to be made to the original strategy. Talbott and Clinton, however, were determined to soldier on. The administration was not about to abandon Russia; nor, as one analyst suggested at the time, to move Russia from being 'the most highly favoured of nations beyond the old iron curtain to being only in the second rank'.[29] Clinton himself made this perfectly clear on his visit to Moscow in January 1994. Indeed, he went out of his way to reassure Russians of America's continuing support and friendship.[30] A few days later Talbott confirmed the US position in an important statement to the House Foreign Affairs Committee.[31] He accepted that Russia was passing through its 'time of troubles', and that 'reformers in Russia were worried and demoralized'. But this was no reason for America to jump ship. In fact, precisely because there was what he called a 'titanic struggle' going on in Russia, in which the United States had a 'huge stake', it was more important than ever to remain engaged.[32] Moreover, according to Talbott, the situation in the former USSR was more 'mixed' than the pessimists claimed. The democratic process was up and running. Over one-fourth of the labour force, he claimed, was now employed in the private sector. In the 'near abroad' there had been some progress too. Even on the security front things were improving: Ukraine had just decided to transfer all its nuclear weapons to Russia, and the US and Russia had agreed to 'detarget' each other.[33]

Talbott agreed that things could still go badly wrong, and felt that the next two-and-a-half years before the elections scheduled for mid-1996 would be critical; however, Russia had not yet passed beyond the point of no return. What the US should not do, he warned, was base its policy today on 'worst-case assumptions about what tomorrow may bring'. This would not only be foolish but could lead the US to 'fall into the trap of the self-fulfilling prophecy'. America thus had to remain patient and continue to work for the integration of Russia rather than begin planning for its future containment. The advantages of doing so were self-evident. A

'Russia integrated rather than contained', he concluded, would 'mean fewer tax dollars spent on defence, a reduced threat from weapons of mass destruction, new markets for U.S. products, and a powerful, reliable partner for diplomacy as well as commerce in the 21st century'. There was still a world to be won.

Criticism of Clinton

If one result of the December 'wake-up call' was initial confusion, followed by a resolute defence by the White House of its original strategy, the other was to open a floodgate for a torrent of criticism. A good deal of this had as much to do with Republican frustrations and right-wing dislike of Clinton as it did with the administration's policy on Russia. Clinton's political opponents, moreover, saw his apparent discomfiture over the Russian question as a golden opportunity to erode his diminishing credibility even futher. The great white shark of Senatorial politics, Bob Dole, was also not insensitive to the fact that by attacking Clinton on such a crucial issue, one upon which the future of his presidency rested, the Republicans might permanently weaken his control of the wider political agenda.

The debate over Russia reached a critical point with the spy case following the disclosure that a senior CIA official had been working for Moscow for several years, apparently with deadly consequences.[34] As one of Clinton's more vocal opponents noted in late February, 'Americans really did not need a major spy scandal to tell them that the honeymoon with Russia was over. But the arrest of the CIA's Aldrich Ames makes the point with some finality.'[35] With this discovery (coinciding as it did with a particularly tough statement by Yeltsin on Russian foreign policy), the attacks against Clinton intensified. One of the Republicans' chief spokesmen on foreign affairs, Richard Lugar, declared that the US had 'to get over the idea' that it was involved in a 'partnership' with Moscow. 'This is a tough rivalry,' he insisted.[36] At the confirmation hearings for Strobe Talbott as Deputy Secretary of State in February 1994,[37] the Republicans launched a bitter attack on what one Senator called a policy which endangered 'our national interests'; they also used the occasion to criticize Clinton's foreign policy more generally. 'If Ambassador Talbott is confirmed by the Senate,' argued Senator D'Amato, 'another wrong signal will be sent: that the people who carry out our foreign policy offer nothing but inexperience and naiveté.'[38]

The politicization of the debate obviously made it difficult for the

White House to concede that its policy towards Russia was in trouble. But there was still a case to be answered. The critics did have a point – several, in fact: that Clinton's strategy was based upon an over-optimistic set of assumptions about Russia's potential to become a stable democratic capitalist country; that it involved too many concessions to Moscow; that although Russia may not at present be a mortal enemy, it was not yet ready for partnership; that American sensitivity to Russian fears about encirclement made it insensitive to East European concerns; and that, although it was reasonable to try to build bridges to Russia, one could not forget the lessons of history, which taught that Russia was more inclined to authoritarianism and imperialism than democracy and friendship with its neighbours.

The case against Clinton was thus a powerful one which logically led some of his more articulate critics, Zbigniew Brzezinski in particular, to some fairly radical conclusions.[39] Since the collapse of the USSR both Brzezinski and his son Ian (now resident in Kiev) had been indulging in what one observer called 'a bit of freelance foreign policy', the primary goal of which was to cultivate links with the non-Russian states of the former Soviet Union.[40] Believing that Talbott's 'romantic fascination with Russia' (Russophilia even) was getting in the way of clear strategic thinking, they made three essential proposals: first, that Eastern Europe should be invited into NATO sooner rather than later; second, that much closer relations should be established with the non-Russian republics, Ukraine in particular; and, finally, that the US should set as its main objective 'the consolidation of geopolitical pluralism' within the former Soviet space. Only through this combination of measures could the United States achieve a more balanced relationship with Russia in particular and Europe in general. Indeed, according to Brzezinski, the creation of a belt of independent states around Russia closely allied to the West would not only serve America's interest, but would help Russia as well; for only when its periphery was secured, and Moscow was no longer tempted to play a spoiling role there, could it become both stable and democratic itself.[41]

Brzezinski's programme was certainly a bold one. Moreover, his proposals had a greater internal consistency than Talbott's insofar as they openly supported the non-Russian nations' absolute right of self-determination. They were also based, to be fair, upon a not entirely inaccurate assessment of the situation in Russia, which by the early part of 1994 looked anything but rosy. The possibility of Clinton actually being converted to the Brzezinski line was of course most unlikely. There was simply too much riding on his original policy towards Russia for him to be so tempted. However, Brzezinski's arguments could hardly be ignored in an increasingly bitter American debate.[42]

Holding the line

Although the Clinton administration was determined not to change course, it was under considerable pressure to modify its original strategy. As a result it introduced a number of small but not entirely insignificant changes to US policy during 1994. For instance, some fairly minor attempts were made to encourage the creation of a network of social services in Russia to cope with the problems involved in moving towards the market.[43] From now on a much greater sensitivity also began to be displayed towards the non-Russian republics. This led (among other things) to an upgrading of relations between the US and Ukraine, a presidential visit to one of the Baltic republics over the summer period, and a series of warnings to Moscow that continuing good relations with the United States presupposed better relations with its neighbours.[44] Finally, during 1994, the rhetoric of the administration changed in a subtle but important way. The emphasis on partnership remained, but this was now tempered by a recognition that Russian and American interests did not necessarily have to coincide perfectly for there to be a normal relationship between the two countries. As Defense Secretary William Perry admitted in March 1994, 'even with the best possible outcome imaginable in Russia, the new Russia will have interests different from ours'.[45]

Having made these adjustments, Clinton (supported by his equally anxious European allies) now took what looked like a diplomatic offensive to draw Russia ever more closely towards the West.

The administration's determination not to break off its engagement with Russia was first reflected in March 1994 when after five days of 'tense negotiations', the IMF finally approved a $1.5bn loan to Moscow.[46] The amount was hardly staggering, and there remained the obvious problem of Russia living up to its side of the bargain by attacking inflation. Nevertheless, the deal was of great importance: not only did it provide the West with continued influence over Russian policy-making, but it signalled Western support for Chernomyrdin and Yeltsin at a time when they were at their most isolated. It also served as symbolic proof (if nothing else) that Russia had not abandoned the cause of economic reform altogether. Indeed, if the IMF had not gone ahead with the loan, it would have amounted to a formal Western abandonment of the reform process. For the time being at least, there were no exits on the rocky road to the market.[47]

The IMF deal was followed in late spring by an equally significant trade agreement between America's economic partners in Europe and Russia. This was important less for what it did and more for what it promised Russia in the not-too-distant future – so long as Russia made some progress towards developing a market economy. As Sir Leon Brittan pointed out at the time, the agreement was 'very ambitious'. It offered Russia the possibility of a free trade pact with the EU, thus marking what he felt was a 'milestone on the road towards greater economic and political stability across the entire continent' of Europe. Moreover, coming as it did at the same time as Russia was moving towards signing NATO's Partnership for Peace, it reinforced Russian links with the outside world. Indeed, Brittan saw a very real connection between the two agreements. The new trade relationship would, he believed, complement Moscow's membership in the Partnership for Peace and in this way enhance Russia's 'ties to the West'.[48]

This was certainly one view of Russia's decision in June 1994 to sign up for the Partnership. Yet few doubted that problems lay ahead.[49] One analyst even argued the Russian decision was just a form of 'great power rivalry' masquerading under a 'pretty name'. Nevertheless, the Clinton administration hoped that over the longer term the move would draw Russa out of its isolation and so reassure the East Europeans that they had nothing to fear from Moscow.[50]

The final act in this rather frenetic four-part play concluded in July when the Russians attended the G7 summit in Naples. Kozyrev, who had been urging the US to revive what he called the 'lagging partnership', was particularly keen for Russia to participate.[51] He hoped and in fact expected that the G7 would one day become the G8. Others were less impressed. One noted Western sceptic dismissed it all as an irrelevant show.[52] Even the moderate Russian reformer, Shokhin, pointed out that the meeting would do little to solve Russia's economic problems. But this missed the point of the whole exercise, which had little to do with economics, and more with the US and its partners reassuring Russia that it deserved a place at the high table alongside the major capitalist powers.

To Chechenia and beyond

These various efforts by both the Russian government and the Clinton administration to stabilize the situation could not eradicate the deeper tensions between the two. Nor could they accelerate the pace of meaningful economic reform in Russia itself, prevent the immiseration of large numbers of ordinary Russians, remove Russia's opposition to NATO expansion, or stop it trying to assert its rights in its own near abroad. Moreover, though there had been obvious changes in the country since the fall of the USSR in autumn 1991, some of these had been more formal than real, and many in fact had made things much worse rather than better, thus leaving the reformists in a highly exposed position. From this perspective, it was particularly worrying to the Americans that the man in whom they had invested so much – Boris Yeltsin – was becoming increasingly unpopular; and that the only way it seemed he could retain power and control over the situation was either by reverting to increasingly authoritarian methods, or by capitulating to those on the nationalist right. Clearly, this was not the smooth transition from the old system to the new one envisaged by the White House back in early 1993.

At least five events confirmed what many now saw as the almost inevitable downward trend in US–Russian relations. The first was internal to the United States itself. With the Republican landslide in November 1994, the political balance in the United States tilted decisively towards the radical right, who were both hostile to Russia and bitterly critical of Clinton's policy towards Yeltsin. They saw only one alternative: to abandon a strategy which had failed and to substitute one that would work. This would involve at least two important policy moves: the speedy expansion of NATO and an increase in US military spending. Only then could the United States look forward to a more stable relationship (not partnership) with Moscow.

The second event was Yeltsin's well-chosen but blunt words delivered at the CSCE summit in Hungary on 5 December 1994, not only reaffirming Russia's opposition to NATO plans to expand eastwards, but temporarily (until May 1995) reversing its decision to sign up for the Partnership for Peace. US–Russian relations, he warned, were at a dangerous crossroads: there was indeed a real possibility that having moved beyond the Cold War, the two were now moving towards what Yeltsin called a new 'cold peace'.[53]

Thirdly, Moscow's decision on 12 December 1994 to invade Chechenia also increased tensions. Though the territory was formally part of the Russian federation (an argument which Clinton apologists used to justify not taking a tougher stand against Yeltsin) the decision to invade, followed as it was by a brutal and vicious war, did a great deal of damage to Russia's image abroad. It also provoked yet another round of intense debate within the United States, which did little to increase public confidence in Clinton's handling of the issue. Moreover, though Clinton himself was not inclined to take action against Moscow, one minor but symbolically important outcome of the Chechen crisis was to stiffen US opposition to Russia's desire to become a full G7 member.[54]

A fourth factor was the Russian decision in early 1995 to proceed with the sale of two light-water nuclear reactors to Iran. The move, not surprisingly, infuriated Republican congressional leaders. Newt Gingrich, for one, warned ominously of 'catastrophic consequences in Congress' if the transfer went ahead. The administration heeded his strong words, but sought to defuse the situation not by cutting off US funds to Russia (much of which was being used to get rid of its nuclear arsenal) but by applying diplomatic pressure. It also pointed out to the Russians themselves that they might 'rue the day' they ever cooperated with a 'terrorist state', especially if Iran built nuclear weapons 'with the benefit of Russian expertise and equipment'. In an effort to prevent the deal going ahead, the Clinton administration took the unusual step of providing Russian officials with US intelligence on Iran. But although the Russians agreed in May 1995 not to go ahead with the proposed sale of a gas centrifuge plant that would have provided Tehran with a supply of enriched uranium, they refused to cancel the $1bn sale of the two nuclear reactors.[55]

Finally, there was continuing friction between the two countries over former Yugoslavia. While Washington saw the conflict as one of Serbian aggression, and backed the Bosnian Muslims, Moscow viewed it primarily as a civil war, and supported Belgrade. And while Russia looked towards the UN and opposed NATO intervention, by 1995 the US had become increasingly disillusioned with the role being performed by the United Nations and argued for a more forceful part to be played by NATO. Indeed, given such differences, it was perhaps fortunate that the Bosnian crisis did not do more to poison relations between the two countries.

Conclusion

The events of late 1994 and early 1995 only seemed to confirm what many had been saying ever since the elections of December 1993 – that if there had ever been a 'honeymoon' in US–Russian relations it was now over. This point was more or less accepted by Russian foreign minister Andrei Kozyrev in March 1995; though he added that although relations between the United States and Russia had entered what he termed a 'sobering period', there was (as yet) no likelihood of a 'divorce'. The relationship would sometimes be difficult and often tempestuous. But there would still be a relationship: a point underscored that same month when the IMF provided Russia with yet another large stand-by loan, in April when the two countries worked closely together to ensure indefinite extension of the Non-Proliferation Treaty, again in May when Moscow agreed at last to sign up for the Partnership for Peace, and finally in July when the European Union signed a long-delayed trade pact with Russia.

But all this was a long way away from the original vision that Clinton and Talbott had shared of building a grand strategic alliance with Russian reform. And with other problems looming on the horizon (some were even concerned about Moscow's commitment to the CFE Treaty and START II), few were prepared to predict how the relationship would evolve over the longer term. There were, of course, powerful factors binding the two countries together. Moreover, in spite of the barrage of criticism directed against Clinton's Russian policy, hardly anybody of note (including Brzezinski) actually seemed to be calling for a severing of US links with Moscow; this simply would not have been in the national interest. Nonetheless, building and maintaining a stable working relationship was turning out to be most difficult, and would almost certainly remain so as the United States moved towards the 1996 presidential election.

Chapter 6

Atlantic rift? The United States and Europe after the Cold War

'Twice this century, America sent its young men to Europe to fight and often to die, for Europe's freedom. It is worth remembering that on neither occasion was communism nor the Soviet Union the enemy. The demise of both will not result in a loss of common commitment since that predated the Cold War and will live on after it. The United States continues to need Europe as much as Europe needs the United States.'
– MALCOLM RIFKIND, *NATO Review*, No. 2, March 1995

The geographical reality of separation between the United States and Europe has only helped obscure the fact that the fate of the two has always been closely intertwined. It was a quintessentially European war between France and Great Britain in the eighteenth century which made American independence possible in the first place. Without general peace in Europe between 1815 and 1914 the United States could never have evolved into an economic giant. And in spite of America's disdain for what it saw as the old diplomacy, each time the balance of power on the European continent was threatened during the twentieth century, it felt compelled to intervene.

In a very real sense, therefore, the United States has never not been a 'European' power. Historically, it grew out of Europe, and later it came back to save the Europeans from their own sins. But it was really the Cold War which made it a European power in its own right, by both entangling it in European affairs and legitimizing its role there to a still isolationist people. There were other, equally compelling reasons, however, that kept the United States in Europe after the Second World War. One, clearly, was economic. Western Europe might have been reduced to rubble after the war, but the United States still had a very real economic interest in the region because of its 'role as a market and as a major source of supply for a variety of products and services'.[1] By closely allying itself with Europe the United States also enhanced its position as a world power. According to one observer, in fact, the US relationship with Europe was critical for US 'global leadership' in the postwar period.[2] Finally, so long as the United States was entangled in West European affairs – and Western Europe was dependent on it for security – it was able to shape its allies' economic choices, their strategic decisions, and their political options.[3]

The Europe which the United States helped construct in opposition to the USSR after 1947 was certainly a good deal more settled than the Europe which Europeans themselves had tried to build after 1918.[4] So settled, in fact, that within a few years of its formation it was generally agreed that the new European system would persist almost indefinitely. Indeed, although the United States remained theoretically wedded to the position that there should be a 'gradual reduction and elimination of preponderant Soviet power from Eastern Europe without resort to war', in practice most policy-makers accepted not only that little could be done to change the status quo, but that the status quo itself actually conferred certain benefits on the United States.[5] A divided Europe, after all, meant a less assertive Germany; a threatened Western Europe was likely to remain dependent on the US; and a Europe controlled by Washington and Moscow could not pursue its own international agenda.

When viewed from this perspective the unexpected collapse of the European Cold War order represented a setback as much as it did a triumph for the United States.[6] It also posed new and difficult questions to which there were no easy or obvious answers.

This chapter looks at the first answer the United States advanced in the shape of a 'new' European security architecture. It then analyses the attitudes of the Bush and Clinton administrations towards post-Cold War Europe. It goes on to assess America's new 'special relationship' with Berlin – and its old one with London. It also considers the vexed issue of NATO and why the United States under Clinton arrived at the controversial conclusion that expansion was both necessary and inevitable. Finally, it discusses the so-called crisis in the Atlantic alliance.

Towards a 'new' European security architecture

The end of the Cold War witnessed the collapse of all Soviet-style institutions in Eastern Europe. It did not, of course, precipitate a parallel disintegration of those Western institutions which had played such a crucial role in undermining the legitimacy of communist power. In America's view it was vital that these remain in being: to hold the West together, to maintain order in a potentially disorderly Europe, to facilitate the transition in the East, and, naturally enough, to secure its own interests in a rapidly evolving situation whose pace sometimes left policy-makers breathless.

The idea of a 'new' security architecture for a new era was first advanced by US Secretary of State, James Baker, in a famous speech in the immediate aftermath of the fall of the Berlin Wall.[7] Though much of what Baker said was provisional in character, it contained, in embryonic form, the main outlines of US policy towards Europe in the post-Cold War period, even after the USSR had collapsed.

The first and most important pillar of the new security architecture was the NATO alliance. On this there was no ambiguity. NATO alone had an integrated military structure. It united potentially competitive states. And its existence, Baker implied, continued to reassure Europeans about Germany's longer term intentions. Moreover, without NATO, the United States would have no organized voice in Europe.[8] In deference to Gorbachev however the United States was careful (at this stage) not to advocate NATO expansion. What was proposed instead was a 'fundamentally different approach' to European security – one based on a vision of 'cooperation' with former foes and not 'coercion'. Only by approaching its old enemy in this way could the US construct a more 'durable European order' without alienating Moscow.

Supporting NATO, and indeed playing 'a central role in shaping the new Europe', would be an increasingly powerful and more integrated European Community.[9] Without it there could be no serious reform in the East. Moreover, when the cycle of reform was completed, it would be to the EC that the new democracies would have to turn.[10] In the American scheme the EC also had the role of anchoring the new Germany into European structures. In effect Baker proposed a new deal in 1989. The United States would support Bonn as it negotiated its way through the diplomatic turmoil caused by the collapse of the Berlin Wall. But in exchange for this support – vital given European sensitivities to the idea of unification – Germany had to maintain its commitment not just to

NATO, but to 'an increasingly integrated European Community'. This was crucial to European stability.[11]

Finally, Baker spent some time discussing the 'new role' of the Conference on Security and Cooperation in Europe, though this was seen as less important than either NATO or the European Community. As Baker noted, after playing its part in setting new political standards before the collapse of Soviet power, it was 'time for the CSCE process to advance further': both in terms of regulating relations between states and institutionalizing human rights as a norm, and as a vehicle for sustaining the 'movement towards democracy' in Eastern Europe. Stalinism was on its last legs: it was up to the CSCE to ensure that in its death throes the communist beast did not wreak havoc.[12]

Bush and Europe

Between Baker's speech and Bush's electoral defeat three years later in 1992, probably more changes occurred in Europe than at any time since the end of the Second World War. Germany was formally united. The USSR disintegrated. NATO undertook a series of major reviews which effectively transformed the Alliance and pushed it closer to the countries of East-Central Europe through the medium of the North Atlantic Cooperation Council. The Maastricht Treaty was signed and the operations of the CSCE were extended and upgraded. But most critically of all the long war began in what had once been Yugoslavia.

The Bush administration won many plaudits for the manner in which it skilfully negotiated its way through Europe's turbulent waters. President Carter's Secretary of Defense, Harold Brown, later acknowledged that Bush had to be commended in particular for the way in which he had handled German unification.[13] Yet there was something instinctively conservative and careful about the Bush policy. In part this reflected his administration's cautious approach to world affairs in general.[14] But there was another factor at work here. Europe was changing so rapidly that Bush feared, quite legitimately in some ways, that American interests might be threatened.

These concerns expressed themselves in at least three ways. First, although the Bush administration genuinely supported deeper European integration, there was an underlying fear that it could have a negative impact on America's economic position. There were many questions to which US policy-makers had no easy answers. For instance, would integration result in increased protection or discrimination against US goods? Would a more integrated Europe not become more competitive, and in turn harm US interests around the world? How acceptable would the EC's generally more social democratic agenda be to US businesses seeking to invest in Europe? In addition, with the move towards European economic and monetary union, would Europe not become far more powerful on the international economic stage – possibly to America's disadvantage? Finally, if a more integrated Europe was less likely to be influenced by US economic conditions, would this not also increase the risk of policy conflict between the two continents.[15]

Economic worries were connected to a second US concern. For the duration of the Cold War there had been no such thing as a distinctly 'European' voice. Europe had remained to all intents and purposes a Europe of the nations – albeit a Europe on the road to acquiring a clearer view of its own collective identity and interests.[16] With ratification of the Maastricht Treaty this was bound to change, and the United States was distinctly ambivalent about this. It might make diplomatic life much simpler. On the other hand, there was a fear that if the Europeans could speak with a single voice, this could have serious consequences, especially if they began to read from a different political script.

A final Bush concern was more specifically military. At one level his administration was in favour of encouraging a greater allied contribution to European defence. It was determined, however, that this should not lead to a separate European defence identity outside NATO. Fears that this might happen came to a head in an (at times) tense debate about the newly created Franco-German corps. Formally launched at La Rochelle in May 1992, the corps gave rise to some concern.[17] While France and Germany reassured the US that the corps would complement rather than duplicate Alliance efforts, Washington regarded the whole thing as dubious at best and potentially destructive of NATO at worst.[18] Bush's Secretary of Defense, Richard Cheney, was clearly concerned, so much so that he urged the German chancellor to abandon the project in 'the interests of Nato solidarity' – no doubt fearing that this very small straw in the wind might, if not carefully controlled, challenge US influence in Europe.[19]

Clinton and Europe

Bush's concerns about the direction in which Europe might go if not carefully 'managed' by the United States were in many ways the concerns which any postwar American president might have expressed. Very much a product of the Cold War himself, Bush still looked at the new Europe with surprisingly old eyes. Of one thing however, he could never be accused: indifference to European affairs. The same did not seem to be true of Clinton during his first year in office. His intellectual preoccupation with economics, and what seemed to some at least to be his geographical fixation with the Asia-Pacific region gave the impression that the United States had almost lost interest – an impression that was heightened by Clinton's failure to visit the continent until early 1994.[20] The suspicion that America was downgrading its relations with Europe was reinforced when Warren Christopher noted in late 1993 that Europe was 'no longer the dominant part of the world', and that US policy hitherto had been far too 'Eurocentric' and from now on would be less so.[21] Though obviously designed to flatter Asian sensibilities at a time when the US was seeking to reinvigorate APEC, both the timing and the message of the speech set the alarm bells ringing around European capitals.[22]

Fears about an American 'tilt' away from Europe during 1993 were followed in 1994 by what now appeared to be a pronounced tilt back towards it. No doubt gauging that US indifference (or its appearance) had done little to enhance American prestige, the administration now bent over backwards to reassure Europe that the Atlantic relationship was as strong as ever, and that the US, in Richard Holbrooke's words, needed Europe every bit as much as Europe still needed an 'active American involvement' to maintain the balance of power on the continent.[23] This renewal of American interest took the form of a series of vigorous interventions.

(i) Presidential

In 1994 Clinton visited the continent on several occasions. This included a high-profile performance at the NATO summit in January, a brief visit to Prague, attendance at the D-Day commemorations in June, and in July official visits to Germany, Poland, Latvia and Italy. In June the President also changed his European team: Richard Holbrooke took over from Stephen Oxman as Assistant Secretary of State, and Alexander Vershbow replaced Jennone Walker at the NSC.

(ii) Europe matters

The revitalization of US policy towards Europe also assumed the shape of a series of major policy statements about Europe's importance. The campaign took off in earnest with the official launch of the Partnership for Peace at the NATO summit in January 1994. But before, during and after the summit several interventions were made by US policy-makers.

For example, the Assistant Secretary of State for Europe, Stephen Oxman, made a speech on 15 November 1993, suitably entitled 'Why Europe Matters'. Secretary Christopher addressed the North Atlantic Council on 1 December on 'A Time of Historical Change for NATO'. Vice-President Gore spoke on 6 January 1994 on 'Forging a Partnership for Peace and Prosperity'. Secretary Christopher talked at the White House on the following day on 'Promoting Security and Stability in Europe'. Stephen Oxman then followed up with at least three other contributions: the first on 27 January entitled 'The United States and Europe: the Year Past, the Year Ahead'; the second on 17 February on 'Building Peace and Prosperity in Central and Eastern Europe'; and the third on 18 April on 'Partnership with Europe is the best U.S. Hope for the Future'.

(iii) European Union

Clinton also used his four trips to reaffirm America's backing for the historic process of European integration. At the US–EU summit in July 1994, he sent the clearest message by any American president of unequivocal support for the process, by stressing his firm commitment not only to the European Union's existence but to a stronger and more self-reliant Europe. To provide follow-up, US–EU expert groups at senior level were set up, charged with making policy recommendations for the next summit in the first half of 1995. Among other issues these expert groups were asked to focus on how the United States and the European Union could jointly strengthen the economies and democracies of Central and Eastern Europe. They were also set the task of examining how the US and the EU could better relate to each other in the new areas of Union competence under the Maastricht Treaty, with emphasis on foreign policy and the fight against international crime and drugs.[24]

(iv) European defence

Moreover, Clinton adopted a far more positive line than his predecessor towards the idea of European security and defence cooperation. In the summit Declaration of January 1994, for instance, the importance of such cooperation and the constructive role played by the Western European Union (WEU) was repeatedly stressed. Significantly, the Declaration included no fewer than eight references to WEU, seven references each to the European security and defence identity, and two each to the Maastricht Treaty and the Union's common foreign and security policy goals.[25]

(v) Partnership for prosperity

Finally, in an effort to reassure Europeans about US intentions, the administration made repeated reference in 1994 to the fact that western Europe was still an area of vital economic interest. Indeed, comparisons began to be drawn between Europe and the Asia-Pacific region, showing that the former was not only economically more important, but in many ways a far more useful economic partner. Thus in one official statement it was pointed out that although the US had roughly the same volume of exports to Europe as to East Asia, it had a positive trade balance with the former and a $75bn deficit with the latter. Moreover, whereas only 17 per cent of all US overseas profits came from investments in Asia, 60 per cent came from western Europe. US firms also had far more invested in Europe ($225bn in 1993) than in East Asia ($60bn). Equally, European companies had much more invested in the US ($258bn) than their East Asian counterparts ($100bn). In short, Europe was not some economic nonentity but America's most important economic partner. Hence everything had to be done to nurture and expand the economic ties between the two continents.[26]

Redefining 'special relationships'

What amounted to a new American compact with Europe also involved a fairly explicit (and to some rather painful) redefinition of America's relationship with different allies inside NATO. Though this process had begun under Bush, it accelerated after Clinton assumed office. Certainly, in a situation where the United States was looking to create a partnership with the EU, it was only natural that it would try to build a closer connection with the one country that was now overwhelmingly dominant within it: Germany.

This new intimacy between Germany and the United States reflected itself in myriad ways. For example, when Clinton wanted advice about Europe from Europeans, it was generally accepted that he would seek it first from Helmut Kohl. Kohl, by the same token, was in constant touch with Clinton. More often than not (and rarely by coincidence) the two also tended to agree on most political questions, including NATO expansion and the need to build a stronger and more integrated European Union. Furthermore, while Clinton's support for Germany enhanced Bonn's status, the close ties worked to America's advantage as well – most obviously when Germany supported US efforts to forge a better connection with the EU. In 1994 this led to the establishment of a series of Euro-American working groups with the explicit goal of coordinating internal security, foreign and East European policies. This was an important step forward for the United States.

Yet while Germany began to play the role of America's new interlocutor in Europe, relations between the US and the UK became visibly less intimate in the post-Cold War era.[27] Aside from the two countries' different perspectives on European integration, at the level of actual policy the decline of the special relationship manifested itself in at least two areas: Northern Ireland and Bosnia.

Basically, before Clinton, all US presidents had treated Northern Ireland as an internal UK issue. Forced to choose between assuaging Irish sensibilities and backing their most reliable NATO ally, American officials (when they thought about Northern Ireland at all) felt they had little choice but to support the British position. After taking over at the White House, Clinton operated under no such statute of limitation, though no doubt domestic considerations also played an important part in his decision to 'intervene' in Northern Ireland. In a serious effort to boost the peace process, Clinton first invited Sinn Fein President Gerry Adams to the United States in early 1994 (much to British dismay), and then pursued a very active policy in Northern Ireland, urged on by the Kennedys but coordinated by Nancy Soderberg in the National Security Council. Finally, to add insult to injury, he invited Gerry Adams back to the White House in March 1995 to celebrate St Patrick's day.

If London was deeply irritated by what it regarded as Clinton's unwarranted interference into matters which did not concern him, it was even more distressed by his various policy initiatives in Bosnia. His moves here, however, should have come as no surprise, for during his presidential campaign, he had raised the question of former Yugoslavia as an electoral issue – accusing Bush in particular of trying to hold the 'dying Yugoslav federation' together and the West in general of failing to do enough to support the Bosnian cause. What exactly either should have done was not clear. But saddled with his original pledge, and under pressure from both liberal interventionists and conservative ideologues to take a stand over Bosnia, Clinton felt compelled to do something more than just accept Serbian gains.

A series of ambiguous statements and threats culminated in November 1994 in the unilateral decision by the United States to suspend its part in the enforcement of the arms embargo against Bosnia. While the consequences of this decision on the ground were minimal, its impact on allied relations was acute and brought to a head simmering differences between the Americans and the British. First, there was deep resentment in London about the way in which the US decision was taken, apparently without any consultation with its friends across the Atlantic. Secondly, the UK saw this move as yet another piece of American posturing more likely to fuel the conflict than to bring it to an end. Finally, the British felt the Americans had no right to take the high moral ground in a conflict in which their own troops were not actually involved.

Perhaps the impact of all this on UK–US relations should not be overstated. But it can hardly be ignored either. On the one hand it left quite a few Americans, including leading Republicans such as Bob Dole, feeling bitter towards an ally which they saw as pursuing a failed policy of appeasement. On the other, it left many in Britain wondering about the United States and its claims to speak for Europe. Comparisons with Suez readily sprang to mind, though in many ways Bosnia had the potential to be far more corrosive. For one thing the situation in the Balkans was more serious. Moreover, there was no longer a unifying Soviet threat to bind up transatlantic wounds.[28]

NATO expansion

The changing character of America's relations with its most important European allies was but part of the wider problem of its attitude and approach to the new Europe as a whole. What exactly was the United States supposed to do on the continent now that there was nothing left to contain? Inevitably this brought the issue back to NATO. Preserving the organization was critical. However, justifying its existence in the absence of a Soviet threat was becoming increasingly problematic. In spite of all the partial reforms it had undertaken since 1989, and the increasingly sophisticated attempts by NATO intellectuals to defend the organization from the charge of irrelevance – an argument which had gained in credence as a result of the crisis in former Yugoslavia – it was patently clear that NATO was developing what one seasoned observer termed an 'identity crisis'.[29]

The ultimate solution to the US dilemma – of both needing NATO and needing to find a post-Cold War role for it – was in the end provided (or so most Americans hoped) by the security vacuum left in East-Central Europe. But the process by which the United States finally arrived at the idea of expansion was a tortuous one. It was certainly not, as Richard Holbrooke subsequently claimed, the 'logical and essential consequence' of the end of the Cold War.[30] Indeed, in the immediate aftermath of 1989 the dominant US view was that NATO should not be enlarged at all, on the then not unreasonable grounds that nothing should be done to weaken Gorbachev's position at home. With the collapse of the USSR two years later, the case for expansion seemed even less convincing. After all, if there had been no reason for enlargement before, why should NATO extend its frontiers now that the other superpower had disappeared?

Ultimately it was not the logic of history but uncertainty and disquiet about events in post-communist Russia that led US officials towards the idea of expansion. But there were numerous problems along the way. Thus when the Partnership for Peace was formally launched in January 1994 the proposal at first was not to extend NATO but, less ambitiously, to strengthen its 'ties with the democratic states' to the East.[31] In fact, under the terms of the PFP no security guarantees were promised or advanced. This provoked a howl of protest among the East Europeans. Indeed, it was partly in response to this that Clinton, in his now famous remarks to the Polish parliament in July, noted that it was no longer a question of 'whether' but of 'when' and 'how' enlargement would take place. However, it was only in the late autumn of 1994 that his administration finally accepted that the PFP had not gone far enough. In October, therefore, it established a 'Working Group on European Security', chaired by Richard Holbrooke, to review the 'how' (though not necessarily the 'when') of the enlargement process.[32] The die, it seemed, had been cast. Urged on by influential voices – ranging from Henry Kissinger and Richard Lugar to the RAND Corporation and the new Republicans in the 104th Congress (who were even keener on the idea than Clinton) – the administration set about selling the idea to its allies.[33]

Those supporting expansion advanced the following apparently irrefutable arguments in its favour: the East-Central European countries could not be left out in the cold; it would enhance democracy in East-Central Europe; the Germans appeared to be keen on the idea; without security in the east there could be no long-term economic stability in the region; the logic of European unification required NATO expansion; and, finally, the situation in Russia remained uncertain. But it was Zbigniew Brzezinski perhaps more than anybody else who put the case most forcefully. NATO, he argued, had a simple choice: either expand or become increasingly irrelevant, wither and then possibly die.[34]

There were many Americans, however, who were less than convinced by these various rationalizations. The influential editor of the liberal journal *Foreign Policy*, for example, suggested that expansion was wrong on at least two grounds: it was extending NATO membership to those who had no reason to feel threatened; and inevitably Moscow would see the move as menacing and 'respond in self-defence'.[35] A former Under Secretary of Defense in the Reagan administration made much the same point, adding for good measure that 'far from solving an alleged crisis, expanding NATO now would fatally weaken' the organization: partly, he implied, because a number of America's allies, including the British and the French, were obviously less keen on the idea than the US; partly because such a move could only work if the United States extended large amounts of economic aid to those seeking to join NATO (which it would not do); and partly because by admitting former Warsaw Pact countries one could easily let in a 'Trojan Horse' which might weaken NATO over the long term.[36]

The case for NATO expansion was also questioned by a number of other experts including Paul Nitze and General John Galvin. They noted that expansion would not only destroy any possibility of constructing a partnership with Russia, but would lead in time to the creation of a two-tier Alliance – with some sitting comfortably under the US nuclear umbrella and others not. Others pointed out that if NATO decided to allow one or two East-Central European countries to join, it would only be logical to let them all in, including ultimately the countries of the former USSR.[37] Moreover, once the implications of expansion became clear, there was no guarantee at all that the US Senate would actually approve the move. One leading Senator was in no doubt about what would happen if expansion came to a vote in 1995. Given the mood of the American people and their increasing reluctance to extend US commitments, 'the answer today would be no'.[38]

The United States thus faced many obstacles as it navigated the NATO ship towards its new port of call. But having decided that the organization had 'to go out of area or out of business', it now had little choice but to live with the consequences of its fateful (some believed fatal) decision. US policy-makers could no doubt comfort themselves with the reassuring thought that expansion was just as much in Russia's interest as anybody else's, and that the United States was not (in Robert Hunter's words) seeking to exclude any nation or draw a new line of division across the centre of Europe.[39] However, this was not how things were perceived by most Russians, and selling NATO enlargement to them would be even more difficult than selling it to the American people.[40]

Conclusion: Atlantic rift?

For the United States the debate about NATO expansion was an attempt to resolve, without necessarily solving, two very basic problems: the larger one of how to build a new security system for the whole of Europe, and the more specific one of how to preserve an organization deemed to be vital to its own interests. But the discussion still left unanswered the question as to where this left US–European relations in general. Indeed, according to one school of thought, America's attempts to keep its banner flying on the continent were doomed to failure: the disappearance of the Soviet threat, what many felt was a US refusal to take a decisive lead in former Yugoslavia, and the emergence of a more self-confident European Union could only lead to gradual separation. And no amount of tampering with NATO, constructing what some saw as worthless architectural designs, or calls for a new transatlantic accord, could prevent this happening. Divorce therefore was almost inevitable.

It would be foolish to underestimate the greater potential for Euro-American disagreement in the absence of a clear and discernible menace to their joint interests. Equally, in an era of geo-economics the competitive side of the relationship was bound to become more pronounced. Indeed, it was precisely in response to such concerns that in the summer of 1995 Washington announced a major effort to strengthen its ties with Europe – a move that would, it was hoped, begin with the removal of trade barriers and eventually conclude with the creation of a Transatlantic Free Trade Agreement.[41]

In spite of these fears and the likelihood of some further drift in the relationship, a real falling out between Europe and the United States was most unlikely, for at least four reasons.

First, in spite of NATO's many transitional problems, there was still a powerful body of opinion sustaining the cause of the Alliance. One of the many interesting aspects of the post-Cold War period was the degree to which support for NATO remained firm. Naturally, the organization could not be expected to be the only pillar of the transatlantic relationship. But if there was one certainty in the new uncertain world order, it was that NATO would continue to enjoy a large degree of backing from elites and publics alike on both sides of the Atlantic.[42]

Secondly, both the United States and Europe shared some fairly basic common economic assumptions. The two obviously had a vital interest in preventing any drift towards protectionism; and in spite of disputes over specific trade matters, both also tended to speak with more or less the same voice on global economic issues. Furthermore, though Europe and the United States championed alternative models of capitalism, these differences were relatively minor compared with those between the economies confronting one another across the Pacific.[43]

Thirdly (and here again the contrast with the Asia-Pacific region was marked), the United States and Europe together faced a common problem in the shape of Russia. On this particular question they were very much united: in terms of the importance they attached to the issue (an importance not always recognized in Japan); in trying to forge a united approach; and in recognizing that if things went badly wrong in Russia, they would have to work out a joint solution.

Finally, although the Cold War may have been a great unifier, we should not forget how often it led to misunderstandings and differences between the United States and Europe. Nor should we forget the cruder varieties of anti-Americanism that had once been a feature of the intellectual landscape in Europe during the Cold War. Thus those who insist today that relations are bound to become worse because the threat has gone would do well to remember that the Cold War sometimes divided allies and peoples as much as it united them. It was not all plain sailing in the good old days.

Chapter 7

The United States meets the Pacific century

'In formulating American policy towards the Asia-Pacific, we should recognize our historical and continuing interests. Since 1784, when the merchant ship *Empress of China* sailed for Canton from New York, the United States has consistently pursued an open door approach towards the Asia-Pacific region. Our interest has resided in maintaining commercial access and preventing the rise of any single power hostile to the United States and its allies and friends.'
– JAMES BAKER III[1]

In Europe the Cold War assumed the form of a potentially lethal but relatively peaceful stalemate. In the Asia-Pacific region, the contest was altogether more fluid and far more deadly. Millions died, including thousands of Americans, in two brutal wars attempting to determine who would control the region's destiny. But in the end, American policy turned out to be a huge success – the first and most obvious measure of which was the emergence by the early 1970s of a viable and dynamic Pacific Rim economy. Usually explained in terms either of a culture of acquiescence, or of the role played by a powerful interventionist state, the economic rise of the Asia-Pacific region would have been inconceivable without the United States. Without the protection it afforded, the aid it extended, or the market access it provided, there simply would have been no East Asian economic miracle.[2]

A few statistics give some idea of the region's economic growth and importance. In 1960 the East Asian economies comprised 4 per cent of the world's GNP. By 1991 this figure had risen to 25 per cent. In the late

1980s US trade with the countries across the Pacific was worth $260bn. By 1993 it had grown to $370bn – 40 per cent greater than US trade with Europe. According to one estimate, almost 3 million American jobs depended on this trade.[3] US companies also had a direct stake in the region, and by 1990 had invested over $60bn there. Moreover, all the projections pointed to further exponential development. The World Bank calculated that between 1990 and the year 2000 the region as a whole would account for 50 per cent of all global growth. Over the same ten-year period, its economic growth was forecast to expand at twice the rate of the United States and three times that of Europe.[4]

The success of the Pacific Rim as an economic project would have been impossible, however, without the creation of key relationships; and the most important relationship for the United States was the one it established with Japan after the Second World War. Indeed, Japan was seen as critical to the reconstruction and development of the region as a whole. An economically dynamic Japan, it was reasoned, would act as a bulwark against communism, a critical market for Asian raw materials and food, and in time evolve into the industrial and technical hub of the region. But to perform these roles Japan literally had to be remade and reformed by the United States. Furthermore, by taking over the defence of Japan, the United States helped reassure Japan's neighbours while providing Japan itself with the security it needed to be able to concentrate its not inconsiderable energies on rebuilding its own economy.[5]

US success in the Pacific Rim can also be measured in terms of the really quite extraordinary change that took place in the relationship with China after Nixon's famous visit to the country in 1972. Having first deemed China to be beyond the political pale, the US finally pursued what turned out to be a far-sighted strategy. This neutralized China as a serious revolutionary threat, helped prepare the way for its re-entry into the world market after 1978, and turned it into a most effective 'ally' against the USSR.[6]

Finally, any assessment of America's historic role in the Asia-Pacific must include a comparison of the region as it was at the beginning of the Cold War – politically most unstable – and as it emerged by the end. Long before the retreat of Soviet power, the region as a whole had been virtually transformed into a model of stability, partly as a result of the active political measures taken by the United States and its allies. Moreover, in the process of fighting communism, the United States pumped billions of dollars into the region (especially during the Korean and Vietnam wars), and these played an absolutely vital role in its economic revitalization.

This chapter argues that the very success of America's long-term strategy in the Pacific Rim – culminating in the collapse of Soviet power – is the principal reason for many of the problems it has faced since 1989. No doubt contradictory policy objectives, and in Clinton's case an overarching ambition to reshape the region, have added to the difficulties of the United States.[7] But in the last analysis these problems are the result, ironically, of its phenomenal success. This argument is explored in more concrete terms in sections on US relations with Japan, China, North Korea and Vietnam. Finally, we look at US efforts to establish an Asia-Pacific community. Though it might be too harsh and premature to suggest that the concept is a myth, there are strong reasons for arguing that it will be a very long time before such an entity emerges.[8]

American success, American dilemmas

The historical success of US strategy along the Pacific Rim has presented American policy-makers with at least five large problems in the post-Cold War era.

The first was how to formulate a coherent policy towards regimes in transition from authoritarianism to democracy – a trend resulting on the one hand from the collapse of communism in Eastern Europe and on the other from the dynamics of capital accumulation in the Asia-Pacific region itself. The United States could only applaud this movement. However, the legitimate yearning for democracy could easily lead (as it did in China in 1989) to political instability. This posed a real dilemma for American policy-makers, in part because they were opposed to disorder as such, but more critically because the measures adopted by countries like China to maintain control at home inevitably led to the abuse of rights which the United States was bound to uphold. Clearly, if Washington failed to act it would be accused of pandering to dictators; but if it stood by its principles, this was likely to compromise its relations with key regimes.

A second dilemma arose over the management of relations with countries with which the United States had been closely allied during (or more precisely because of) the Cold War. This posed a very specific challenge in the case of China, which had long exploited its privileged role as an anti-Soviet asset to construct a very 'special relationship' with the United States. But it also created major problems in terms of American ties with Japan. For having been a virtual dependency, Japan now found itself in the strange, and perhaps rather exhilarating, position of no longer requiring US protection from the USSR. Inevitably this made Tokyo less deferential to Washington. Some leading figures were now even prepared to say 'no'. But, not surprisingly, in this new environment, where national security was no longer the overriding concern, the United States also became more critical of Japan and started to attack economic policies which it had previously encouraged. Inevitably, these attitudes led to a souring of US–Japanese relations.[9]

This was particularly noticeable in the economic sphere. Here again the dilemma for the United States was the result less of failure than of success. For having laid the foundations for capitalism in the region as the best defence against communism, the most effective means of generating economic growth, and the least dangerous (or costly) way of advancing its own material interests, the United States now found it had to come to terms with the consequences, one of which was a new economic self-confidence, displayed not only by the smaller tigers like South Korea, but also by the biggest tiger of all, Japan. The emergence of a Japanese economic superpower would have been problematic enough. What made it appear even more so was the perception at home that the American dream had finally come to an end. A mood of unease began to spread during the late 1970s. Temporarily driven underground by Reagan's self-confident rhetoric during his first term, it then resurfaced in the last days of the Cold War with the publication in 1988 of Paul Kennedy's hugely successful and influential study, *The Rise and Fall of the Great Powers*. Though attacked for overstating the degree and extent of US decline, the book captured a feeling that America was going the way of all empires, and might even one day be overtaken by its most obvious and successful rival across the Pacific.

The sense of unease was further exacerbated by the collapse of Soviet power. Though a welcome development, it raised a number of critical issues – one being about America's continued commitment to the region's security. Many wondered whether, faced with no observable challenge to its interests, and confronted at home by pressures to cut costs by closing US bases in the region, America might one day disengage from East Asia completely. Such a move, it was feared, would upset the whole balance of power in the area, encourage other powers (such as Japan and China) to be more assertive, and even lead to a new and destabilizing arms race.[10]

The final American dilemma flowed directly from the failure of communism. By the end of the 1980s, the contradictions of communism in Vietnam had created a major problem in the form of nearly a million refugees. In China the movement towards economic decentralization threatened the country's very integrity.[11] And the systemic decay of the North Korean regime had the potential to upset the stability of the whole region.[12] Containing communism when it had been in an ascendant phase had been difficult enough. Dealing with the results of its decline could turn out to be just as problematic.

The Japanese 'threat'

The Bush administration attempted to define a new approach to Japan.[13] This was based, in essence, upon the notion not only that US–Japanese relations should assume a more equal character, but that the two countries should actually cooperate to form what James Baker in June 1989 called a new 'global partnership'.[14] Indeed, he proposed a quite stunning vision of a close association between the two nations.[15] This partnership, he pointed out, would work to their mutual economic advantage; it would contribute to peace and stability in the Asia-Pacific region; and it would permit the two countries to cooperate on wider global issues. Recognizing both the degree of economic interdependence between the two powers, and the enormous international possibilities if the two could work in tandem, the United States under Bush seemed to look forward to a mutually beneficial, almost intimate working relationship with Japan.[16]

This vision did not collapse so much as become increasingly irrelevant after 1989. Instead of US–Japanese relations entering a more cooperative phase, the opposite happened. There were several reasons for this (including the Gulf war) but one factor above all triggered the crisis: the almost irresistible rise of a large trade imbalance between the two countries. To the Japanese this was a mark of their own economic vitality; most Americans took a somewhat different view and blamed the situation almost entirely on Japanese trade practices. But one group in particular went further, arguing that the deficit was not merely a product of policy, but rather the reflection of deep structural problems within the Japanese system. These so-called 'revisionists' fairly rapidly managed to shift the whole focus of the discussion away from a simple exchange of views about trade, towards a far-reaching debate about Japan as a particular type of society – one which was not only different, but so difficult to change that a radically new US approach was required to defend the West against Japan's drive for economic supremacy.[17]

This shift towards a more confrontational American approach reached its climax with the election of Clinton in 1992. His administration's definition of American foreign policy as an almost 'head to head' strug gle for world economic domination; the espousal by some of its theoreticians of a fairly overt form of economic nationalism; and the recruitment into the administration of economists such as Laura Tyson who had written at length about the threat posed by Japan in the area of high technology – all suggested that stormy days lay ahead.

Clinton's more aggressive approach took the form of pressing Japan, on threat of retaliation, to import specified quantities of certain US goods. The aim was to shock the Japanese into taking effective action and, in turn, to increase the US share of the Japanese market. It would also, he hoped, 'converge Japan's international accounts with the rest of the international economy' and by so doing give a much-needed boost to world trade.[18] Finally, by taking what looked like effective measures against Japan, Clinton obviously expected to win popular support at home. To this degree at least, talking tough on trade with Tokyo had as much to do with winning credibility in Congress as with winning contracts across the Pacific.

Talking tough, however, was one thing: getting results was something else.[19] Thus although the so-called 'framework' agreement signed by Clinton and Prime Minister Miyazawa in July 1993 looked like a breakthrough, it did not in fact specify a numerical goal to reduce the surplus as the United States had demanded.[20] In February 1994 the Japanese (now led by Morohiro Hosakawa) again refused to commit the government to numerical targets.[21] In frustration the United States came back for a third time in spring 1995, this time over the issue of US imports of Japanese cars. But once again, it found itself in a difficult position. Indeed, by threatening to impose a 100 per cent tariff on Japanese luxury car imports, it managed to upset not only Tokyo but also the European Union, which protested forcefully. In fact, so confident were the Japanese that they could win this particular battle that they threatened to seek a ruling against the United States from the newly established World Trade Organization.[22]

How do we explain what amounted to a series of American retreats and compromises? One reason was determined Japanese resistance to American pressure. As a former Japanese diplomat put it, 'the Americans found the Japanese nut too hard to crack'.[23] Of equal significance was the fact that Japan could count upon support from the wider international community, including the European Union, which saw America as trying to grab a bilateral advantage in Japanese markets.[24] Nor could Clinton mobilize full domestic consent for his policies. Some opposed what they saw as his 'myopic' adoption of 'managed trade'.[25] Others were concerned that his strategy, which seemed to be driven almost entirely by the Commerce Department, would weaken the still important political and military ties between the two countries. It was significant, in fact, that during 1995 the Departments of both State and Defense took active measures to correct the impression that economics alone shaped relations between Tokyo and Washington.

Clinton's policy, moreover, though driven by a simple economic logic, was in at least three senses economically illogical. First, even if Japan had done far more to assuage American demands, this would have had very little effect in reducing the US deficit. For if Japan was a successful trading nation, this had less to do with high tariffs than with the fact that it was (as one American report pointed out) a 'country with fierce competition, low taxes and inflation, intact families and a strong education system'.[26] Furthermore, what Clinton seemed to be demanding was almost impossible for any Japanese prime minister to concede: partly for domestic political reasons (especially at a time of great economic trouble at home) but also because it would have amounted to a virtual surrender of economic sovereignty to the United States. Finally, his policies could eventually have eroded the very foundations of a world trading system of which the US was part and from which it could not escape. Clinton, in effect, was economically trapped. The danger was that, faced with continuing demands to 'do something', he might just try to escape the trap – with devastating consequences for the rest of the world.[27]

Images of China

According to one seasoned observer, 'Americans have long portrayed China in overly simplistic ways, either in exaggerated positive terms, or else overstating the negative'. Thus before the revolution the country was viewed almost romantically, after 1949 with almost fanatic suspicion, and then post-1972 in an increasingly positive way that reached a climax during the second half of the Carter administration. But the pendulum did not stop swinging. For the greater part of the 1980s, many Americans enthusiastically embraced China as an ally against the USSR and the first communist state to experiment seriously with capitalism. However, after the Tiananmen Square massacre in June 1989, several observers began to look at China as some sort of rogue nation whose economic success had been made possible only because of the repressive and exploitative nature of a system that was resistant to political reform.[28]

Although US policy towards China during the 1990s has revealed many of the same pendulum-like qualities – seeking on the one hand to maintain normal relations with an increasingly powerful country and on the other to uphold some core American values – this should not lead us to the conclusion that the United States has had no strategy at all.[29] Three goals have driven US policy since 1989.

The first has been to promote economic reform in China while attempting to accelerate the country's further integration into the world economy. A China on the road to capitalism, it was argued, was likely to be a more responsible member of the international community than one which was not. A prosperous China with a liberal economy, moreover, would provide an important market for US goods and services. And a China that was undergoing rapid economic development had more chance of developing in a pluralistic direction than one that was stagnant and moribund. Indeed, one of the most important American arguments against isolating China (one accepted by both Bush and Clinton) was that by doing so the US would only reinforce the authoritarian tendencies it was seeking to weaken. Far better, therefore, to engage China and in this way encourage the trend towards democracy.[30]

The second policy goal has been political. Even if China had not constituted the fastest growing economy in the world, there would still have been considerable merit in maintaining close relations with it because of its sheer size and potential, its diplomatic leverage, its position as a permanent member on the Security Council of the United Nations, and the fact that it remained a nuclear weapon state.

Finally, the United States still had to be sensitive to the balance of power in the region. Russia, after all, still possessed serious military capabilities. Japan was a major economic force which might one day decide to translate its material strength into political power. There was also a chance that if, or when, Korea was finally united, it too would pose a more serious political challenge. Thus the US had a vested interest in maintaining good relations with a China that helped counter the likely pretensions of other powers in the region.

US policy towards China since the end of the Cold War was thus somewhat less incoherent than has normally been suggested. Even so, there were a number of areas of important disagreement. Though none was critical enough to undermine what US policy-makers regarded as a crucial relationship, they were serious enough to complicate it badly – so badly in fact that by June 1995 Beijing was warning that 'Sino-US relations' were 'once again at the crossroads'.

(i) Economic issues

As much as 40 per cent of Chinese exports (worth roughly $37bn) went to the United States in 1994 – obviously giving the United States enormous leverage in any trade negotiations. Trade disputes continued to complicate relations after 1989. The most important source of contention was China's growing trade deficit with the USA. In 1989 this stood at between $5bn and $6bn. A year later the figure had risen to $10bn, and by 1993 it was close to $23bn.[31] There were other sources of economic friction, especially over Chinese piracy of American computer software, films and other intellectual property. This delicate question was finally resolved in February 1995 after the US threatened to impose punitive tariffs on a small percentage of Chinese-made goods. Winston Lord, the US Assistant Secretary of State for East Asia and Pacific Affairs, later confirmed in a speech in Beijing in March that the settlement of this issue was a step towards China being allowed to join the World Trade Organization. Previously, the United States had actively lobbied against such a move.[32]

(ii) Human rights

Trade disputes were of less importance than China's denial of human rights. Clinton was especially vocal on the issue. Yet, having raised the question in his electoral campaign of 1992, two years later he was compelled under pressure from US multinationals (and most foreign policy experts) to delink human rights from the annual extension of most-favoured-nation (MFN) status. The decision clearly caused some anguish within the American administration, with reports of the State Department under Warren Christopher lining up on one side of the debate and the Department of Commerce under Ron Brown siding with US business interests on the other. Clearly, if MFN had been denied it would have had massive repercussions for Sino-American relations. A retreat was therefore almost inevitable. But as Clinton's National Security Adviser Anthony Lake later pointed out, Washington would not permit the issue of human rights to go away.[33] In fact, in early February 1995 the State Department issued its Human Rights Report in which Assistant Secretary David Shattuck stated that there had been no improvement in the situation in China during the previous year.[34]

(iii) Chinese military power

China was both a nuclear 'have' and an exporter of arms to other countries. By the late 1980s it had also become a military power in its own right. This did not threaten the United States directly: indeed, most Western experts continued to regard China's military forces as being second- or even third-rate. Nonetheless, there was still some cause for American concern. During 1994, for example, Chinese military spending rose by about 20 per cent with plans for further increases. At the beginning of 1995 its admittedly outdated airforce had become the third largest in the world. China also had a growing navy. It laid claim to the entire China Sea (including the Spratly Islands). And the People's Liberation Army was at least a potential problem, given that China had border disputes with at least seven neighbours.[35]

(iv) Taiwan

Although relations between Taipei and Beijing had improved quite dramatically (for instance Taiwanese trade with and investment in mainland China had blossomed since the late 1980s), there were outstanding problems which necessarily involved the United States. Beijing, for instance, still refused to rule out the use of force against the island should it veer towards formal independence; and, through strong-arm tactics, continued to prevent Taipei playing an international political role. The situation was further complicated by the fact that Taiwan continued to enjoy strong and vocal support from conservatives in the US Congress. Moreover, the mid-term elections in November 1994 produced a majority in both the House and the Senate that was likely to be far more critical of mainland China on such issues as trade, human rights and its policy towards Taiwan. When in February 1995 the new speaker of the US House of Representatives, Newt Gingrich, gave his backing to Taiwan's entry into the United Nations, China was incensed.[36] It became even more incensed following the 'private visit' to the US by Taiwan President Lee-Teng Hui in June. And what might have been a diplomatic victory for Taipei caused one of the worst flare-ups in relations between the US and China since full normalization in 1979.

North Korea: from containment to engagement

Nowhere perhaps was the Cold War more tense than on the Korean peninsula. Here two deeply opposed and highly armed powers confronted each other across the 38th parallel with little or no prospect of the conflict ever coming to an end. Even after the fall of the Berlin Wall and the symbolically important unification of that other country divided by the Cold War, the best that could be expected was perhaps a less dangerous stand-off, rather than any genuine settlement of outstanding issues. But inevitably the events in Eastern Europe and the Soviet Union began to have an impact on what US policy-makers still regarded as a very dangerous situation on the Korean peninsula. Initially, these epochal shifts in the international environment led to a partial improvement, but after 1992 relations between North Korea and the US deteriorated badly – that is, until the United States reached agreement with Pyongyang on 21 October 1994.

There were basically four dimensions to the short-lived rapprochement in the early 1990s. First, the end of the Cold War transformed the diplomatic landscape. Formal relations were established between China and the USSR (1989), the USSR and South Korea (1990) and South Korea and China (1992). There was a corresponding breakdown in relations between Pyongyang and Moscow and strains began to develop between Pyongyang and Beijing.[37] Secondly, in contrast to the success of the South Korean economy, the North's economy continued to stagnate and the end of the Cold War only made this worse. In March 1993 Russian and East European diplomats in Pyongyang revealed that between 1990 and 1992 the North Korean economy 'may have plunged by as much as 7–10 per cent'. The fear of a sudden economic collapse in the North may have been one of the factors motivating Seoul to open discussions with the North.[38] Thirdly, two major agreements – on political reconciliation and on the denuclearization of the Korean peninsula – were signed between the two Korean governments in December 1991. Finally, in early 1992, six years after it had signed the Nuclear Nonproliferation Treaty, North Korea reached agreement with the International Atomic Energy Agency on an inspection programme designed to confirm that its nuclear programme was for peaceful uses only. US and North Korean officials met at policy level in January 1992 – the first time since the end of the Korean war. Starting in April 1992, IAEA officials conducted six inspections of North Korean facilities.

Thereafter the situation began to deteriorate badly. Efforts to implement the 1991 accords between the two Koreas stalled. Confrontation also escalated on a number of fronts between IAEA inspectors and North Korean officials. Then on 12 March 1993, the North announced its intention of withdrawing from the NPT, presumably to avoid inspection requirements of the treaty verification. This led to intense negotiations between the US and North Korea during 1993. In March 1994, Pak Yong Su, the chief delegate at an inter-Korean meeting, stated that the proposed UN sanctions would prompt North Korea to unleash a 'sea of fire on Seoul. Fortuitously perhaps, Kim Il Sung died on 8 July 1994, opening the way to a negotiated settlement of the nuclear issue and removing at least one of the roadblocks to the introduction of economic reforms within North Korea itself.[39]

The US strategy during this second very critical period was shaped by five considerations:

(1) To eliminate the North Korean nuclear capacity. Secretary Perry, in testimony to the Senate Foreign Relations Committee on 24 January 1995, admitted that US forces had given 'serious consideration' in 1994 to destroying the North's 'nuclear weapons facilities'.[40]
(2) To enforce the NPT – especially important in the lead-up to its summit in the spring of 1995.
(3) To preserve US security relations with the Asia-Pacific region. Many US officials speculated that if North Korea had actually acquired a real nuclear capability, Japan might have been induced to respond in kind. Brent Scowcroft later argued that one of the main reasons for ensuring a non-nuclear North Korea was to prevent Japan and others from thinking about going nuclear.[41]
(4) To encourage North Korea out of its dangerous isolation. As Perry noted on 3 May 1994, North Korea was at a 'crossroads not just on the nuclear issue but also on the future of its relations with the rest of the world'.[42]
(5) To send the clearest message possible to the North that it would meet with a massive response if there was a serious breach of the peace. The wider issue of US credibility was at stake here.

After months of what Warren Christopher later described as 'determined diplomacy and negotiation' the 'Agreed Framework' was finally signed. The 'US goal in crafting the agreement', he argued before the Senate Foreign Relations Committee in January 1995, was threefold: 'to stop the North's existing nuclear program; to devise a larger strategy that would address the threat posed by the North's missile program and conventional build-up; and to reduce tensions in the region by bringing North Korea out of its international isolation into the broader community of nations'.[43] In concrete terms the agreement froze the North Korean nuclear programme. North Korea also agreed to dismantle its nuclear facilities in a phased manner. In return the United States arranged for an international consortium – the Korean Energy Development Organization – to build two light water reactors, and made arrangements to supply heavy oil, beginning in January 1995: 50,000 tons in the first year, 100,000 in the second, and 50,000 tons annually thereafter to compensate North Korea for energy production lost as a consequence of abandoning its gas graphite reactors. In addition, the United States committed itself to reduce barriers to trade and investment within three months and to exchange liaison officers. Finally, it provided security assurances against the threat or use of nuclear weapons against North Korea.[44]

There were, however, many problems with the agreement. It was easily reversible. The world also had to live with the possibility that North Korea had a nuclear capability for an extended period of time. Equally troubling was the apparent lack of a larger strategy for reducing tensions on the Korean peninsula. Moreover, there was concern that by signing up to the agreement, the US ran the risk of strengthening a decaying and ultimately doomed system. According to one former American official, 'by throwing an economic lifeline' to North Korea Washington had unwittingly reinforced 'the dangerous habits of the old regime'.[45]

Such criticisms led many US analysts to conclude that the Clinton administration would have real problems in getting endorsement for the agreement at home, particularly from the new Republican-dominated Congress. Jim Hoagland analysed the dilemmas better than most. In his view, apart from the fact that North Korea was being rewarded for breaking an earlier agreement, and the regime itself was being saved from possible collapse, there were three other questions which administration officials had to answer. First, did they really believe that North Korea had 'ceased being a backlash state and should therefore be trusted?'; secondly, 'why did Kim Jong Il do the deal now?'; and, thirdly, would the agreement not 'serve as an incentive for other backlashers to pursue nuclear weapons programs to get bought off by the United States?'. But Hoagland also noted that the agreement posed very real problems for Pyongyang as well. As US officials pointed out in private, the economic and political concessions being offered were 'in fact poisoned bonbons': the North would have to open up to such a degree that this would lead to the erosion of the system. Unfortunately, such subtle long-term thinking might not carry the day with Congress or the American people. There was still some 'hard selling to do at home'.[46]

In fact, at Senate hearings conducted in January 1995, the architects of the deal had a relatively easy ride. There seemed to be no alternative to the agreed policy, and the agreement itself defused an extremely tense situation. Most importantly, it did at least hold open a door through which the North Koreans could walk if they so chose. This was critical. By early 1995 there was a general consensus that the end of the Cold War meant that change was now virtually inevitable in the North. The question was now when and how this would happen – and with what consequences. For all its flaws, the agreement of October 1994 provided a framework within which those problems might ultimately be resolved.[47]

Vietnam – the last domino?

When Vietnam finally fell to communism in 1975 there was a widely held assumption that the other 'dominoes' in Southeast Asia would soon fall as well. But the opposite happened and Vietnam was left as one of the few remaining communist outposts in the Asia-Pacific. One of the poorest socialist countries in a booming capitalist region, it was perhaps only a matter of time before the winds of change sweeping the world in the late 1980s would impact upon Vietnam. Yet improving relations with United States was never going to be easy. Vietnam's continued occupation of Cambodia, the domestically charged issue of Americans missing in action in the Vietnam war, and the deep hostility of the US towards a regime which had done so much to destroy its international credibility in the late 1960s and 1970s meant that the path back to normality was likely to be strewn with rocks and boulders.

The United States first imposed a trade ban on Hanoi in 1964 and then extended it to the whole country in 1975. Under the terms of the draconian 'Trading with the Enemy Act', individuals caught breaking the embargo, or even spending more than $100 a day while visiting Vietnam, could be fined up to $1m and given ten years' imprisonment. In addition, the United States blocked lending to Vietnam by the World Bank, the International Monetary Fund and the Asian Development Bank. It enforced the trade ban and the credit block with the utmost seriousness – to such a degree that as late as 1990 one analyst could still write of Vietnam being 'cut off from the West by a ruthless US aid, trade and investment embargo'.[48] The overall impact of this economic warfare upon Vietnam was probably less than many of its critics claimed. Nevertheless, it made it virtually impossible for Hanoi to gain access to international lending institutions, and of course kept US business out of Vietnam.

The ending of the US embargo came at the end of a long series of important changes both within Vietnam and between Vietnam and the outside world. They fell into two main categories: economic and diplomatic.

(i) Economic

Stagnation at home, the economic example of the other Southeast Asian countries, and reforms introduced by Gorbachev in the USSR finally persuaded the Vietnamese Communist Party of the need to implement its own form of perestroika (*doi moi*). The changes, introduced by Party leader, Nguyen Van Linh at the 6th Party Congress in 1986, aimed to encourage the growth of private business and small business enterprise. In 1987 the regime then introduced a surprisingly liberal investment law designed to attract foreign investment. Two years later it entered into negotiations with the IMF, after which it implemented tough monetarist policies. The communist collapse in Eastern Europe and the USSR further accelerated the process of reform by cutting Vietnam off from its main source of aid and trade.[49]

These various changes did not revolutionize the Vietnamese economy overnight, but did have a measurable effect at home. They also led to a steady growth of foreign direct investment. By 1989 this stood at a little under $400m; by 1991 it had risen to $1.94bn, and by 1992 to $2.8bn (one-third of it by oil companies). By 1993 foreign companies had been granted licences for more than $6bn worth of projects.[50] Yet American-based companies could not invest in or trade with Vietnam, and in 1990 only 43 American businessmen visited the country. As foreign competitors became more involved in Vietnam, large US corporations in particular (including IBM, General Electric, BankAmerica, Citibank and Caterpillar) began to place pressure on the US government to change its policies. The American Chamber of Commerce in Hong Kong took the lead in lobbying for relaxation of the embargo. The business community also had supporters in Congress including the influential Richard Lugar, for many years chairman of the Senate Foreign Relations Committee. In the early 1990s a number of US companies undertook pilot studies and started to set up shop in Vietnam – but could do nothing serious while diplomatic relations remained frozen.[51]

(ii) Diplomatic

In April 1991, the State Department outlined a four-stage process for normalizing relations with Vietnam. The signing of the Cambodian peace agreement in October 1991 was the first step. For the second – after a ceasefire had been agreed and the UN transitional administration established in Phnom Penh – Washington would partially lift its trade embargo. The third phase would start after six months of UN administration in Cambodia. In this phase, the trade embargo would be lifted and Hanoi and Washington would exchange diplomatic missions. Finally, in the fourth phase, Washington would establish full diplomatic and economic relations after elections in Cambodia, scheduled for early 1993.[52]

Following a key meeting between James Baker and Foreign Minister Nguyen Manh Cam of Vietnam in Paris the following October, relations between the two countries began to improve. In April 1992, a US ban on telecommunications was lifted. Then, on 14 December 1992, President Bush signed an order permitting US companies to conclude contracts with Vietnamese parties and open offices in Hanoi – in anticipation that the ban on doing business with Vietnam would eventually lapse. In February 1993, President Mitterrand became the first Western leader to visit Vietnam since 1975. Finally, in the same month, a group of American executives from some two dozen companies visited the country under the auspices of the new Vietnam–American Chamber of Commerce.

By the time Clinton became president, therefore, the situation was rapidly changing. Nonetheless, Vietnam had to wait another year before the embargo could be lifted and another two at least before the US decided to re-establish diplomatic relations. Indeed, American caution became all too apparent at the annual meeting of the Asian Development Bank in May 1993 when the US alone refused to countenance ADB loans for Vietnam.[53] Further pressure from US business forced Clinton to make more concessions in September, but for political reasons – primarily to do with his own war record and the vexed issue of American servicemen missing in action, he was not prepared to lift the embargo completely. By December, however, a consensus seems to have emerged within the administration that it was now feasible to move forward, and in February 1994 the embargo was lifted. Even so, the sensitivity of the issue compelled the White House to draw a distinction between lifting the embargo – which made sense economically – and establishing normal relations.[54] For some the Vietnam war may have been brought to a conclusion by the ending of the embargo. But for others – including the nation's veterans organizations and the many families of those whose relatives were still missing in action – there could perhaps be no end to the longest war in America's history. And though diplomatic ties between the two countries were finally restored in the summer of 1995, many suspected it would take even longer before Hanoi and Washington could establish a 'normal' working relationship.

Conclusion: towards an Asia-Pacific community?

The end of the Cold War did not, of course, imply an end to America's role in the Asia-Pacific, but it did leave it without a broader purpose. Moreover, unlike in Europe, there were no ready-made structures like NATO or the CSCE through which it could shape the region's destiny. It thus had to think seriously about its relationship with the area as a whole, and try to construct some form of architecture that would both advance its own interests and ensure it could still shape the Asia-Pacific agenda.[55]

The collective agency the United States decided to utilize to achieve these goals was APEC. But it was not entirely clear what exactly Clinton or his aides hoped APEC would achieve – or become. Some assumed it would evolve into a vehicle that would one day create a sense of political community where none existed at present.[56] Others were less certain. But there was general agreement that APEC was about economics. As Clinton himself pointed out, APEC was about 'the jobs and futures and incomes of the American people'.[57] Winston Lord made the point with equal bluntness: 'The fact is this is the most dynamic region of the world ... if we are interested in more exports and jobs, the most lucrative direction is the Asia-Pacific region'.[58]

The United States set two other goals for APEC. The more general one was to make the organization 'a driving force' for trade liberalization worldwide. In this way the initiatives taken in Seattle in November 1993 and confirmed at the APEC summit in Indonesia a year later would act as 'catalysts for new global trade negotiations to maintain the momentum of liberalization'.[59] APEC's other – and more difficult – purpose was to open up Asia itself.[60] Although most countries along the Pacific Rim generally welcomed America's reinvigorated commitment to the region, many wondered where this might lead over time.[61] For instance, many shared China's uneasiness about Clinton's apparently strong views on human rights, seeing this basically as an unwarranted attempt by the US to impose Western standards on Asian cultures. Others, notably Malaysia, were also wary that the United States was seeking to establish a privileged position for itself. In fact, Dr Mahatir Mohammed, the Malaysian Prime Minister, boycotted the Seattle summit, claiming that it was designed to ensure American domination of the Asia-Pacific region.

Thus there was, from the outset, a deep suspicion that in spite of its veneer of communitarianism, APEC was little more than an American organization with an American agenda. Hence, US attempts to turn it into anything other than a loosely constituted consultative group with minimal authority to set trade and investment policy, were likely to meet with deep reistance. But this only reflected an even deeper problem for the US as it sought to define a role for itself in the Asia-Pacific region. For the better part of forty years the United States had dominated the area, in ways which would have been almost unthinkable in Europe. Now this most diverse of regions was finally coming of age. Although it still needed the United States as both economic dynamo and military stabilizer, it did not always appreciate US leadership. Moreover, any attempt by the United States to lead was just as likely to produce a 'self-defensive Asian reaction' as obedience or compliance.[62] In the new Pacific order 'Asians', it seemed, no longer wanted to see 'Asia used as a means for American ambitions'.[63] If this was the case then APEC – which looked a suitable vehicle for the realization of such goals – was unlikely to achieve its full potential.

Chapter 8

Whatever happened to the Third World?

'Why America helping Afghanistan
when Russians here and not now?
Where our American friends now?'
– ASADULLAH, a 53-year-old Afghan
working for the Afghan Red Crescent[1]

It is perhaps remarkable that two of the most brilliant studies on American foreign policy – one written by a Marxist and the other by a former Reagan official – should come to almost identical conclusions about the critical role played by the Third World in the Cold War. Naturally, to the radical Gabriel Kolko and the far more conservative Peter Rodman, the moral high ground in the great struggle was occupied by different actors. Kolko, moreover, was drawn towards a materialist interpretation of US policy; Rodman, on the other hand, viewed the Cold War confrontation as essentially a moral and strategic contest between the opposing ideologies of Leninism and Wilsonianism. But there the disagreements ended. Both accepted that what had begun in Europe just after the Second World War was really fought out in Europe's former colonial possessions in Asia, Africa and Latin America; that the bloody contest which then followed had immense implications for the global balance of power; and that whoever won in the Third World would be able not only to shape the fate of the vast majority of humanity, but indirectly to determine the future of the core regions. For whoever could control the 'countryside', as Guevara once referred to the Third World, would in time be able to control the 'towns' of the metropolitan regions as well. The stakes along the so-called periphery were clearly enormous.[2]

Clearly, winning the Cold War in the Third World was every bit as important for the United States as holding the line in Europe; and this chapter looks at what 'winning' has meant for US foreign policy since 1989. It examines first what the end of the Cold War has meant for the Third World in general and four regions in particular: Africa, the Middle East, Latin America and South Asia. It then goes on to analyse US aid policy in the post-Cold War period, and concludes with a discussion of what some observers have called the soft foreign policy issue of global environment.[3]

The United States and the Third World in the Cold War

Given its anti-colonial origins and its stated opposition to European colonialism, one might have assumed that the United States would have become the champion of the emerging nations after 1945. In fact, despite formally supporting the principle of self-determination, and managing to build reasonable relations with at least some of the new regimes in the ex-colonial countries, there was always an underlying tension between the United States and the emerging Third World. Although some historians have explained this in terms of an American misunderstanding of the nature of nationalism, or a more basic cultural blindness tinged with racism, there were objective factors underlying the antagonism.[4]

One reason for the hesitancy of the United States in embracing the new radical nationalism was its general inclination to put the economic and political needs of its recovering and still vulnerable West European allies above the aspirations of those struggling for independence in Asia, Africa and the Middle East.[5] As a result, the United States was placed, or placed itself, in the invidious situation of underwriting (or appearing to underwrite) European control of countries whose independence it formally espoused. Although this policy was not without its contradictions (witness the Suez crisis), it left the United States open to the not unreasonable charge of betraying its own anti-colonial heritage.

Secondly, there was a very real fear that if the underdeveloped countries adopted radical policies this would weaken the West economically, by leading to an increase in key commodity prices such as oil, or to a reduction in market access, or to a loss of Western control over critical strategic raw materials. Washington was also disturbed by the economic programme adopted by many of the new elites in the less developed countries. In essence, the United States wanted an open world economy within which all countries obeyed the same rules. Many nationalists, on the other hand, saw a necessary conflict of interests between their own goal of rapid economic development and remaining part of this multilateral free trade system. They also emphasized the central role of the state and state planning in fostering economic development, whereas the United States saw the solution to economic growth in terms of free enterprise and private property.[6]

Thirdly, many of the new governments in the Third World were influenced by and attracted to the Soviet economic model. In the USSR, after all, industrialization had been autarchic and particularly swift, and had led to the creation of the same sort of heavy industrial base which planners in many underdeveloped nations saw as the key to economic independence and full development.[7]

US concerns about the Third World were reinforced by the fact that many of the most effective radical nationalists were either communists themselves (as was the case in China, Cuba and Vietnam) or were closely associated with local communist parties tied to the Soviet Union. In South Africa, for instance, over half of the African National Congress leadership by the mid-1980s were members of, or closely associated with, the South African Communist Party.

Finally, as a superpower with an anti-imperialist mission, the USSR was particularly well placed to support national liberation movements, and did so to some effect from the late 1950s onwards.[8] Espousing an ideology which was more anti-Western than genuinely Marxist, it achieved early successes in the Middle East, until its expulsion from Egypt in 1972. It also extended its largesse to (and its influence through) the Castro regime in Cuba, the Vietnamese Communist Party, the Dergue in Ethiopia, the MPLA in Angola, Frelimo in Mozambique and the Sandinistas in Nicaragua. Indeed, it is unlikely that some of these regimes could have survived or endured as long as they did without Soviet backing.[9]

The United States thus had good reason for concern, and in pursuit of its goals utilized several instruments. These included foreign aid, land reform, military advice, the arming and training of armies and anti-communist guerrillas, and, when all else failed, direct military intervention (a less favoured option after the Vietnam war). Some presidents (Carter, for instance) preferred supporting reform and aligning with the cause of radical change, rather than standing against it.[10] Most, however, were principally concerned with order, and were sometimes not bothered about the type of regime they were prepared to underwrite so long as the outcome was favourable to American interests. But whatever the means deployed, the Cold War had a marked impact upon the Third World. Nearly 20 million people died in 'limited wars' fought there. The high level of conflict inevitably increased the power and influence of the military. This in turn weakened the already weak impulse towards democracy and distorted the development process. But a high price was also paid by the United States – in terms of American lives lost, democratic ideals betrayed or not realized, and the creation of a culture of intervention.

The end of the Cold War: in stages

The Cold War in the Third World reached its climax in the late 1970s. Fred Halliday makes the telling point that whereas 'no state fell to revolutionary forces' between 1962 and 1974, 'no less than fourteen countries, across the whole geographical span of the tropical south' fell to the left between 1974 and 1980.[11] The causes of this were primarily internal to the contries concerned. But international factors – US decline in the wake of Vietnam, a greater Soviet willingness to project its influence, Cuba's desire to enhance its status abroad, and the collapse of the Portuguese empire in Africa – also contributed to these revolutionary successes. What also lent credibility to the then fashionable argument that the Third World had finally come of age was an improvement in the South's economic position as a result of a favourable shift in the terms of trade.

This surge of revolutionary and economic optimism collapsed in the 1980s. Long before the winding down of the Cold War proper the situation had changed dramatically, to the advantage of the West in general and the United States in particular. First, the revolutionary wave of the 1970s started to ebb, in part because the Reagan administration took the offensive against a number of the new left-wing regimes. Many policy-makers in the USSR also began to question the cost-effectiveness of supporting radical regimes in the Third World. At the same time the balance of economic power shifted as a result of a marked fall in primary commodity prices. Finally, a number of countries which had previously espoused the cause of economic nationalism and planning (Mexico being the most significant) were forced to rethink their policies – partly for domestic economic reasons, but more obviously because of the external pressure placed upon them by the IMF as a result of their deep indebtedness to the West. This pressure led to a widespread abandonment of traditional left-wing strategies and the adoption of more orthodox economic remedies. The president of the World Bank, Barber Conable, summed up this shift in 1990, arguing that the most remarkable thing about the past decade was the acceptance in many underdeveloped or developing countries that 'market forces and economic efficiency were the best ways to achieve the kind of growth which was the best available antidote to poverty'.[12]

Thus even before the collapse of communism in Eastern Europe, the Third World challenge was already in retreat, though until 1989 at least US policy-makers continued to attack what President Reagan had earlier characterized as Soviet support for 'terrorism, insurgency and aggression' in 'strategically sensitive regions'.[13] With the passing of the Cold War this support evaporated, as did the very idea of communism as an alternative ideology. The combined impact of all this upon the Third World was immense.

(1) After 1989 a number of revolutionary states either collapsed, were overthrown, or were simply elected out of office. Among those to fall were the regimes in Afghanistan, Ethiopia, South Yemen, Angola, Mozambique and Nicaragua.
(2) Without Soviet backing many other states, such as Cuba and North Korea, found themselves in an increasingly isolated position, facing the strong likelihood that they would not be able to survive over the long term.
(3) The collapse of planning as an economic model in Eastern Europe and the ex-USSR further undermined the case for it in the Third World. Many communist regimes – notably Vietnam – also began to experiment in a more serious way with the market.
(4) The end of the Cold War forced a sea-change in the ideological orientation of a number of national liberation movements. This was perhaps most marked in South Africa, where the ANC effectively abandoned its previous proposals for full-scale nationalization of the economy. This in turn helped prepare the way for a final settlement, culminating in the elections of April 1994.[14]
(5) With the USSR (and later Russia) acting in a cooperative rather than a hostile way, the path was also cleared for negotiated settlements of other outstanding regional conflicts. The Israeli–Palestinian accord of 1993, for example would have been unthinkable in an earlier era. (So, too, would the IRA ceasefire in Northern Ireland in autumn 1994. For even though the Provisional IRA owed no loyalty to the USSR, its leaders were influenced by the general trend away from the armed struggle in other parts of the world, in particular in the Middle East and South Africa.)
(6) Finally, the fall of communism in Eastern Europe and the USSR accelerated the intellectual decomposition of Marxism in the Third

World. What had once been the dominant paradigm among a large section of the intelligentsia in the less developed countries effectively collapsed.

Farewell to the 'Third World'?

By any measure, the great sea-change of the 1980s and early 1990s represented a significant breakthrough for the United States. It left the world more open. It reduced the likelihood of regional conflict involving either superpower. And it enabled the United States to bask (for a while) in a new-found ideological self-confidence. It also provided Washington with an opportunity to recast its policies towards the less developed countries. Moreover, the way was now open for the United States to abandon some of its less savoury clients and to push ahead with serious democratic reform.

But what sort of 'Third World' now existed as US policy-makers looked forward to this brave new world? Did it exist any longer as a recognizable entity? In some ways it obviously did. Nearly all of the countries within the 'Third World' had experienced European colonial rule. The inhabitants of these countries were not white. Most of them were extraordinarily poor. And in spite of rapid change, there remained an apparently unbridgeable economic chasm between the countries of the 'South' and the economic haves of the 'North'. To cite the simplest statistics, while three states with only 9 per cent of the world's population (Germany, Japan and the United States) accounted for over half of world income, Latin America, Africa and South Asia together, with over 30 per cent of the world's population, accounted for only 10 per cent.

The term still had its uses, therefore. But it also obscured as much as it illuminated. It lumped together countries which, having perhaps been equal in the 1950s, were now at very different levels of development. By 1989, the newly industrializing Asia-Pacific countries had very little in common with, say, the nations of sub-Saharan Africa or Central America. By the same measure, what, if anything, united the oil-rich states of the Middle East with resource-poor Peru or Guatemala? Moreover, the term 'Third World' had not merely defined an area but prescribed an alternative form of development to that laid down by Western economic orthodoxy. The notion also presupposed antagonistic 'First' and 'Second' worlds between which the 'Third' could manoeuvre. Again, by the 1980s, all this had changed. There were now no longer three separate worlds operating according to different laws, but an integrated world economic order. To many in the Third World this was a recipe for de-industrialization and even deeper poverty as they struggled to implement IMF and World Bank policies. But to most US policy-makers this new situation was altogether more acceptable than what had existed before. The world was now whole again.[15]

The myth of imperial temptation

The end of the Cold War represented not only a triumph for the market but, according to some analysts, the beginning of a new phase in the history of American imperialism.[16] One writer talked of a new American crusade utilizing democratic rhetoric as its philosophical cover. Two others even went so far as to talk of a 'colonial revival', with the United States, like some late-twentieth-century Cecil Rhodes, virtually leading the advanced Western countries back into the heart of the underdeveloped world.[17]

This argument, given momentary credence by Bush's rhetoric in 1991 about a 'new world order', in fact pointed in almost the opposite direction to the one in which US policy began to travel. Far from being tempted to new crusades, the United States began to display if not a total reluctance to intervene – Panama after all was liberated in the same year that communism collapsed in Eastern Europe – then at least a certain lack of confidence or purpose in doing so.

First came the Gulf war: a highly effective military action in an area of vital interest, but one which turned out to be as much an exercise in self-restraint as proof of America's still awesome military capacity. It certainly did not overcome any Vietnam syndrome as Bush claimed at the time. This was followed soon after by 'Operation Restore Hope' in Somalia.[18] Here the US intervened so ineffectively, and with so little obvious intention of staying, that the long-term result was to make Americans less, not more, inclined to deploy their forces abroad in the future. Proof of this was provided a year later in another part of Africa. In Rwanda the United States not only failed to intervene in early 1994, but to forestall any public pressure to do so it at first appeared to deny that the Hutus were actually engaged in 'genocide'.[19]

Of course, the liberation of Haiti might be read as clear proof of America's new imperial ambitions. Here, after much debate, a great deal of political intrigue, and an eleventh-hour 'intervention' by former President Jimmy Carter, US forces were finally dispatched to the island in September 1994. Ostensibly sent to restore a by-now impatient and a less radical Aristide to office, this limited (and as it turned out rather successful) police action in America's backyard was, however, roundly condemned by nearly everybody at home, from those on the conservative right such as Jeanne Kirkpatrick, through to the more liberal *New York Times*, which put the post-Cold War realist case against the US action most succinctly. While accepting that the previous regime was 'morally and legally reprehensible', it concluded that there was no justification for invasion when there was no 'clear threat to vital American interests or to international peace'.[20] In his equally scathing critique Peter Rodman also raised the spectre of other interventions, including the one in Somalia, warning Clinton that though it might be easy to get into Haiti it could prove far more difficult to get out.[21]

Out of Africa

The question of interest, or more precisely what interest the United States actually still had in the Third World, was raised in a particularly acute form in sub-Saharan black Africa. Previously, when there had been a perceived revolutionary threat to the region, the United States had no difficulty in justifying its role there. Indeed, it had propped up some of the worst regimes in the world in Africa in the name of anti-communism.[22] But now the only substantial reasons for involvement were humanitarian, or to promote democracy.[23] Communism had been seen off in Ethiopia, Mozambique and Angola, and the left had virtually disappeared. Black Africa could now be put – as Peter Schraeder has argued – onto America's 'back burner'.[24]

The increasingly marginal character of black Africa in American calculations was reflected in a number of ways. There was, for example, a reduction in the numbers working in the State Department's Bureau of African Affairs. US consulates and embassies were closed in at least four countries. The US Agency for International Development also had to cut a number of programmes and staff positions.[25] In addition, the already very low level of US aid going to Africa was further reduced, some part of it in 1990 even being transferred to Poland. By the early 1990s Africa was receiving only 8 per cent of American aid (about $800m) – and this in a continent of nearly 600 million people.[26]

Significantly, though, while its interest in black Africa diminished, the United States continued to follow events in the other parts of the continent very closely. It had good reason to do so. Sudan had recently become an Islamic fundamentalist state. Algeria was being torn apart by a brutal civil war between Islamic militants and a secular government.

Egypt was under threat. Libya was a designated terrorist state. And South Africa was a major economic power in its own right, which in 1992 was identified by the US Commerce Department as being one of the twelve 'Big Emerging Markets' in the global economy. In the same year, black Africa accounted for only one per cent of world industrial output – a 200 per cent drop from 1970.[27]

Peace in the Middle East?

America's apparent lack of interest in black Africa stood in sharp contrast to its still close (almost intimate) involvement in the affairs of the Middle East. Here, as leading official Dennis Ross noted, the decline of the Soviet Union had had an enormous impact on the nature of the region as a whole. It had weakened the position of those opposed to American influence. It had permitted a 'previously unthinkable degree of co-operation' between the United States and the USSR, enabling the former first to isolate and then to defeat Iraq in the Gulf war. It had also reduced Israel's strategic importance in US eyes. And finally, it had cleared the way for a new regional dialogue between both Israel and the PLO and the United States and Syria. This led to the important Madrid Conference of late autumn 1991, followed two years later by the signing of a Declaration of Principles by Israel and the PLO, committing them to a new peace process. Though the peace deal was initially brokered by the Norwegian government, clearly the key international players behind the final signing were the United States and Russia – a point forcefully driven home a month later when the two jointly sponsored a critical conference in Washington to support the 'Middle East Peace'.[28]

America's continued engagement in the Middle East reflected the region's pivotal importance in the wider global system. It was, after all, the site of the largest recoverable deposits of crude oil in the world, and a valuable and valued market for US companies – especially those involved in the still important arms trade. There was also the issue of America's long-standing commitment to the integrity of Israel (endorsed and reinforced by a powerful Jewish lobby in the United States itself). Lastly, there were a number of regionally significant actors in the Middle East who were not only opposed to the United States, but were also a very real threat to key allies whose security ultimately depended on American backing.

America thus had good reason to remain involved in the region – one obvious measure of which was the high level of aid it continued to give to Israel and Egypt. Despite the anti-aid mood in Congress, in 1995 between them the two countries were still receiving $5bn per annum – about 40 per cent of all US foreign aid disbursed that year.[29]

Yet, in spite of victory in the Gulf war and the peace settlement between the PLO and Israel, the Middle East remained extraordinarily volatile, and one of the most likely sources of any future conflict involving the United States. First, there was the ever-present and growing danger of Islamic fundamentalism. Having captured Iran in the late 1970s, just under twenty years later it threatened the still fragile peace process in the Occupied Territories. Secondly, whereas Israel was willing to make peace with the PLO, it was not willing to stop the building of settlements along the West Bank, bring its own right-wing militants under control, or sign up to the Nuclear Non-proliferation Treaty. Finally, Washington faced not one but three backlash states – Iran, Iraq and Libya – all of them oil-wealthy, and each one with the resources necessary to continue to defy American political demands.

Good neighbours? Hemispheric relations after the Cold War

Perhaps nowhere in the Third World had the challenge to US hegemony been as intense as in South and Central America. Here a powerful combination of anti-imperialism and extraordinary disparities of wealth made for a highly volatile situation where radical ideas found a ready audience – one which inevitably grew following the Cuban revolution of 1959. The American response was to contemplate reform, but meanwhile to take political shelter behind a number of very brutal military juntas. Washington responded in much the same manner to the revolutions in Central America in the late 1970s, by giving aid and comfort to those whose main claim to US support was not their democratic credentials so much as their proven capacity to contain and defeat the challenge of Marxism-Leninism.[30]

The period immediately prior to the end of the Cold War, however, was a highly contradictory one for Latin America. On the one hand the continent witnessed a gradual but measurable increase in the number of countries claiming to be democratic. On the other it experienced the worst recession in Latin American history since the 1930s. Thus by the time the USSR decided to disengage from Eastern Europe, the region was in massive debt (about $400bn p.a.) and per capita income was lower than it had been thirty years previously. Naturally, the collapse of communism in Europe did little to alleviate the hemisphere's economic woes.

But it did have a marked impact on the political situation. Nicaragua and Cuba were left to their fate (the Sandinistas being voted out of power in spring 1990). Marxism more or less disintegrated as a serious intellectual project. And a political space was created in which it was now possible for domestic elites to permit even greater democratic expression. By 1992 in fact only one regime in Latin America could properly be described as a dictatorship.[31]

Washington's attempt to define a strategy for itself in this new environment bore a marked similarity to the one it had pursued with uneven success in the 1980s: encouraging market-style reforms, integrating the region more completely into the global economy, fostering greater internal economic integration, and promoting the cause of democracy. The difference now was that there was a much better chance of achieving these related goals.[32]

In this grand strategy Mexico was regarded as a flagship for the rest of the continent. First, the increasingly close ties between Mexico and the United States would, it was argued, serve as a model for the type of good relations the latter aimed to have with all its neighbours in the hemisphere. Secondly, if the economic changes introduced in Mexico could generate sustainable growth, this would inspire others to go down the same reformist path. In this context the passage of NAFTA was especially important, because it was hoped the agreement would not only promote reform in Mexico, but act as a powerful stimulus to all reformist Latin American leaders to intensify their efforts to restructure their economies and societies. By fostering what the United States saw as normal relations between itself and Mexico, NAFTA would also reduce the Latin American need for US economic support. In the past the continent had looked to its powerful ally in the North primarily as a source of aid. Now America's main role would be to stimulate growth on the continent by engaging with Latin America economically. Trade, not aid, was seen as the path to genuine hemispheric prosperity.[33]

The American approach to Latin America thus focused almost exclusively on two main issues: economic and political reform, and developing the continent as a secure market for US exports. On this there was no real disagreement between Bush and Clinton, though it was Clinton who worked particularly hard to enhance American economic access to the region. In 1993, for instance, he directed US officials and other senior advisers to study ways in which trade could be increased throughout the Americas. He also pressed for the establishment of various sub-regional agreements which his administration hoped would act as economic building-blocks for Latin America as a whole. Certainly, the Commerce Department had very high expectations about the continent. In 1992 US exports amounted to just over $75bn and the plan was for this figure to increase three- or fourfold by the year 2000.

Nevertheless at least four issues still concerned US policy-makers. One of the biggest was the fact that so few seemed to be benefiting materially from all of these changes. According to official figures, about 45 per cent of the population were still living in abject poverty in 1993. Capitalism in Latin America did not wear much of a human face – and where there were inhuman conditions ordinary people could still be driven to revolt (as they were in the Mexican state of Chiapas where the peasants obviously preferred Zapata to NAFTA). A second worry was that in spite of economic reform, many countries remained financially vulnerable (again, as was revealed in Mexico, where the peso crisis not only threatened the country's economic stability but impelled US politicians, regardless of party, to extend a $40bn loan guarantee to the government in early 1995). Thirdly, the issue of Cuba remained unresolved. Here the US faced the double problem of both encouraging gradual reform on the island and at the same time convincing Cuban exiles in Miami that it remained resolutely anti-communist. Finally, though the left in Latin America no longer represented a direct political threat to US interests, the region's profound internal difficulties menaced the United States indirectly in the shape of imported cocaine and large numbers of increasingly destitute would-be immigrants. These challenges could hardly be compared with those Washington had faced during the Cold War. But their very existence meant that American policy-makers had to remain actively involved in the region: benign neglect was not an option.[34]

South Asia

During the Cold War the US had few serious economic ties with South Asia, though the region was of immense strategic importance, inevitably enhanced in US eyes following the Soviet decision to invade Afghanistan in 1979. In this sensitive area, however, Pakistan and not neutral India was America's chosen instrument, performing what one observer has termed 'an assortment of dubious services for the US'. After 1954 it fronted a fairly meaningless regional alliance for Washington (SEATO). The U2 pilot Gary Powers took off from Peshawar on his disastrous flight in 1960. Henry Kissinger used the country as a discreet go-between with China after 1969. The CIA's multi-billion-dollar proxy war in Afghanistan was channelled through Pakistan's powerful intelligence agency, the Inter-Services Intelligence (ISI). Pakistan also became home to two million Afghan refugees.[35]

With the ending of the Cold War (symbolized as much by the Soviet decision to withdraw from Afghanistan as the fall of the Berlin Wall) the political landscape changed in South Asia almost overnight – to the disadvantage of Pakistan. Having indulged its different leaders as useful allies in the days of the Soviet threat, the United States now began to distance itself from Islamabad; in late 1990 it abruptly stopped new military and economic aid to the country (worth about $560m) because President Bush felt unable to assure Congress that Pakistan did not have a nuclear weapons capability. Concerns about Pakistan's nuclear status grew when American intelligence discovered (probably some time in 1991) that the country was also involved in helping Iran develop a nuclear capability of its own. According to well-placed sources, Tehran launched a crash five-year nuclear plan in the wake of the Gulf war, aided by Pakistan's then chief of staff, General Mizra Aslam Beg. The row dragged on until the government of Benazir Bhutto finally halted all nuclear cooperation with Iran in early 1994. This prepared the way for a thaw between the two countries that culminated in a visit by the Pakistani Prime Minister to Washington in April 1995, followed a short time later by a US Senate plan to ease the original sanctions.[36]

A number of issues, however, continued to complicate the relationship, particularly Pakistan's refusal to sign up to the Nuclear Non-proliferation Treaty. There was concern, too, that Pakistan still had the potential to be a dangerous source of expertise for other Islamic countries interested in developing a nuclear device. Moreover, though the United States sought to remain neutral between Pakistan and India, it was worried about Islamabad's involvement in the Indian state of Kashmir, fearing that this might impact on the territorial integrity of India as a whole.[37]

In general terms, therefore, the end of the Cold War made Pakistan less useful and the United States critical of its former allies' nuclear programme. By the same token it helped pave the way for a real improvement in US–Indian relations. The fact that India had a much longer record of genuine democracy than Pakistan made this transition much easier. It was in turn helped by the Indian government's decision in 1991 formally to abandon its 40-year-long search for planned economic self-sufficiency – a move forced upon it by a mounting debt crisis (India by then being the third largest debtor nation in the world) and the loss of

Soviet economic support. In turn, the collapse of the Soviet Union – India's greatest ally in the Cold War – and the failure of its own brand of 'Nehruvian socialism' impelled Delhi to rethink its more general position in the world. Almost inevitably this led to a reassessment of its previously frosty relationship with the United States.[38]

The improvement in relations was symbolized by an official six-day visit to the United States in May 1994 by India's Prime Minister P.V. Narasimha Rao – the first such visit since Rajiv Gandhi's in 1987. This exercise in bridge-building was no doubt helped by the fact that the United States had by then become the largest non-oil exporter to India and its single most important source of foreign investment (since reforms began in 1991 American companies accounted for over 42 per cent of foreign investment proposals). It was further enhanced by the Clinton administration's identification of India as one of the 'Big Emerging Markets' whose potential had only barely been tapped.[39]

But the road to normalization was by no means a straight one. Thus although there had been significant economic reform in India and an improvement in its economic relations with the United States (in 1993 US investment totalled $1bn and its exports $4.5bn), much still needed to be done to convince US investors that India was a worthwhile and a safe place to put their money. The issue of confidence was brought into sharp relief indeed when the state government of Maharashtra decided to review the $920m Dabhol power-station project in spring 1995. This was a particularly critical decision, for the project was the biggest ever involving an American company in India. Both Indian officals and the US ambassador to India, Frank Wisner, sought to play down the potential damage to commercial relations. But in spite of this, it was clear that the state government's review managed to generate considerable international concern.[40]

In addition, the Kashmir question continued to fester. India on the one hand was deeply irritated by continued US criticism of its army's behaviour in the Himalayan state. The United States on the other was disturbed by what it saw as Indian disregard for human rights. Washington was also worried about India's military capabilities, in particular about Delhi's determination to push ahead with the development of both the *Prithvi* (its short-range missile) and *Agni* (its intermediate-range ballistic missile).[41] It was naturally even more concerned by India's refusal to sign the Nuclear Non-proliferation Treaty.

But underlying this in turn was a deeper long-term fear about relations between India and Pakistan. The two countries had gone to war during the years of the Cold War, and there was not yet any visible sign of an improvement in the relationship. US efforts to mediate had come to nothing and the possibility remained that at some time in the future the two might go to war again, this time with far more deadly results. As Clinton's first Director of the CIA, R. James Woolsey, observed, if nuclear war ever happened then the most likely place was South Asia. For this, if for no other reason, the United States had to remain engaged in the region.[42]

The twilight of foreign aid?

The most successful US initiative after the Second World War had little or nothing to do with its possession of the atomic bomb, its massive airforce or impressive navy, but was the result of a decision it took in 1947 to extend a helping hand to others. Indeed, by supporting the West Europeans through the vehicle of the Marshall Plan, the United States not only laid the foundations for their successful rehabilitation, but by so doing helped undermine the legitimacy of Soviet power in Eastern Europe over the long term. A simple but supreme act of 'enlightened self-interest' thus changed the course of history.

Nevertheless foreign aid was never particularly popular in the United States. Identified by a some as a hand-out to foreigners, by others as socialism by the back door, and by many as a complete waste of money, the only way it could be legitimized was in terms of its value as a weapon in the Cold War. That was how the Marshall Plan was sold in 1948 to a then parsimonious Congress; and it was the way in which nearly all foreign aid was justified thereafter.[43]

Naturally, with the passing of the Cold War, it was inevitable that the already weak case for foreign aid would become weaker still. With no threat left to contain, it was increasingly difficult to persuade the average American that helping others was still in the US national interest. This opposition was reinforced by other powerful factors; these included America's own economic problems, a widespread belief that aid had done little or nothing to encourage development in the Third World, the widespread perception that the country was spending far more on aid than it actually was, the growing power of Congress and, finally, the intellectual ascendancy in the West of a modern version of neo-classical economics whose influential practitioners stressed the importance of markets over government decisions in determining the allocation of scarce resources in the world.[44]

Under such circumstances it was imperative for the executive to rethink the purpose of foreign aid – partly to protect it from the even deeper cuts it was likely to be subject to by Congress, but more obviously because a new mission was needed to justify foreign aid to a public keener to solve America's problems than those of others. The future direction of foreign aid was briefly addressed by Bush.[45] However, the real job was left to the Clinton administration and the new head of USAID, Brian Atwood. Faced with sharp budget cuts (the foreign-aid budget had already been slashed by about a half since its 1985 peak of $26bn) and an overburdened organization, Atwood set out to define a simpler and clearer set of goals. In the end four were identified as vital: the building of democracy in the Third World, the protection of the environment, the fostering of sustainable development and the encouragement of population control.[46] But as Atwood and others emphasized, foreign aid could not be viewed in isolation from America's broader international objectives.[47] There would certainly be no free hand-outs. Moreover, when aid was disbursed, particular account would be taken of its impact on the health of the US economy. Aid which advanced American economic goals would find ready favour: aid merely intended to alleviate poverty would not be viewed as sympathetically.[48]

Furthermore, although lawmakers themselves accepted that foreign aid should reflect the dramatic changes which had taken place in the world, few were prepared to devote a great deal of time to the subject; and when they did it was generally to call for even deeper cuts than those that had already been made or proposed. After the mid-term elections of November 1994, the administration found itself up against a majority in Congress which appeared to regard foreign aid as little more than a massive international welfare programme.[49] This was somewhat ironic, for the United States by then was spending only $15–16bn on foreign aid (in the same year its military budget was over fifteen times larger). Furthermore half of that was going to Israel, Egypt, the countries of Eastern Europe and the former USSR. In real dollar terms the United States in 1995 was probably spending only 15–20 per cent of what it had expended forty-five years previously. It was a sign of changing times, however, that as foreign aid continued to fall, opposition to it seemed to grow more shrill.[50]

The politics of virtue and the Third World

While foreign aid slipped down the US foreign policy agenda, other questions came to the fore during the 1990s. It would be unwise to exaggerate their salience to US policy-makers. But Washington was now prepared, or compelled, to engage with issues it had not considered important before. These issues were criticized by some as reflecting the concerns of a politically correct, prosperous North rather than the needs of the poor South, but their emergence nonetheless deserves brief mention here.[51]

Flying down to Rio

The idea of sustainable development was not a new one, but it finally acquired international status and recognition when the UN Conference on Environment and Development (the 'Earth Summit') was held in Rio de Janeiro in June 1992. The largest gathering in history of presidents and prime ministers addressed almost every conceivable environmental issue – from global warming and biological diversity, to population control and deforestation. The so-called 'Agenda 21' which emerged from two years of preparatory work was a long and complex document. Comprising 40 chapters, it was without doubt the most far-reaching programme of action ever approved by the world community. Some even referred to it as a comprehensive blueprint which, if ever implemented, would effect an irreversible transition to sustainable development.[52]

The final Rio Declaration, however, really satisfied nobody. The environmental lobby saw it as a fudge, while many of the richer nations signed up to it (or so it seemed) because they had little intention of doing much to implement its many provisions. The United States supported the Declaration, but with the proviso that it might seek a reopening of the debate. It had a number of major problems with the Declaration. For one thing, it did not like those parts of it which appeared to lay the blame for environmental damage almost entirely at the door of the wealthier countries in the North. It also objected to that section which referred to the 'right to development', fearing this would lead to economic rights being put above human rights. It feared, too, that environmental concerns might be used to justify protectionist policies. Finally, the United States refused to sign up to the Earth Summit's treaty on biological diversity. For these reasons many were highly critical of its role at Rio: lecturing the poor South about its birth-rate, yet contributing more to global pollution than any other nation while doing little in real terms to alleviate world poverty. Some environmentalists, indeed, were utterly sceptical of Washington's commitment, seeing William Reilly (administrator of the Environmental Protection Agency and the chief US delegate to the Rio conference) as a lonely voice within a Bush administration that appeared to be more interested in protecting US interests than defending Mother Earth.[53]

A Green in the White House?

If the Bush administration had its doubts about the outcome of the Rio Summit, some in the incoming Clinton team had none about the importance of environment as a global and human issue. Al Gore had already written a large book on the subject.[54] Published in the same year as the presidential election, it was seen by many as a very positive sign, though other, less sympathetic commentators were alarmed by Gore's deeply spiritual (at times almost metaphysical) statement on behalf of the environment. Drawing upon historical and religious evidence, he argued that the modern scientific method had encouraged a Cartesian divide between man and nature, science and religion which had led directly to a high level of toleration of environmentally destructive activity. He proposed a 'Global Marshall Plan' to deal with the crisis. This was imperative. For over forty years the US had expended its energy in containing communism. It was now essential, he concluded, that it commit itself in the same way to meeting the equally serious challenge posed by the environment.[55]

Gore's call for a new and more serious American approach to global environmental problems certainly forced the issue higher up the US foreign policy agenda, but it did not lead to the release of fresh funds to pay for his bold vision. In 1991 USAID officials estimated that the agency had 'obligated' some $663m to address environmental questions (40 per cent of which went to Egypt).[56] Four years later it was spending about the same amount, with little prospect of any increase. Thinking big about the planet was all very well; translating these grand ideas into policies was something else. In an age of economic insecurity, few seemed prepared to make the sort of sacrifices or changes in life-style demanded by Gore.

Conclusion

As the discussion above has shown, it is clear that immense and apparently irreversible changes in the very nature of the Third World have led to important alterations in US foreign policy – though not always to the benefit of some of the less developed countries. For instance, these countries have found it increasingly difficult to manipulate US fears and strategic needs to their own advantage. They have also suffered from the reduction in US aid. And although US-sponsored market reforms may bear fruit over the longer term, the people of the Third World will still have to cope with the inevitable pain involved in moving from a system that was protected and orientated towards social welfare to one that is open and competitive.

For its part, the United States cannot afford the luxury of ignoring what transpires on the 'periphery'. In spite of its miniscule trade ties with black Africa, and its limited economic relations with the nations of South Asia, economically the less developed countries are important – and are likely to become more so. Furthermore, though there is no longer a Soviet threat, politically there is still a great deal at stake in the Third World. For instance, if the process of democratization were to stumble and fall, this would represent a major setback for the United States. Moreover, policy-makers need little reminder that the most serious threats to the United States mainly derive from the Third World problems: the Third World after all is the primary source of global terrorism; all of the so-called 'backlash states' are located there; and the problem of nuclear non-proliferation arises mainly because of Third World resentments. For all these reasons, the United States has no real alternative but to remain actively involved. And perhaps a little more involvement now might save it considerably more grief later.[57]

Chapter 9

Conclusion

This book started with a question and a challenge. The question was, basically, what was a superpower like the United States supposed to do without another superpower to fight? And the challenge was to those who have argued that US foreign policy has been incoherent since the end of the Cold War in general and Clinton's election in particular. As I hope the preceding discussion has shown, the picture is not quite as dismal or as chaotic as critics claim. Beneath the surface of everyday political reality one can detect a reasonably clear set of goals which have been pursued since 1989: to reduce foreign policy costs where possible; to encourage the broad historical movement towards democratic capitalism around the world; to compete more effectively in the world economy; to deter aggression by maintaining a reasonable military capability; to underwrite the balance of power in both Europe and Asia; and – though more implicit than explicit – to ensure that the United States remained the dominant actor in the international system.

This list of broad objectives confirms the truism (noted in the Introduction) that US interests have not changed as much since the end of the Cold War as some analysts imply. The best example of this was provided in our discussion of post-communist Russia. Here, although US policy has clearly undergone a radical shift, the United States continues to see Russia, as it did between 1947 and 1989, as its primary security problem. By the same token it still has a vital interest in the affairs of Europe, the Pacific Rim and the Middle East. And although some might wish otherwise, as a superpower with a wider international role to play it has also not abandoned one of its most cherished notions, derived from practical experience during the Cold War: that stability in an anarchic world ultimately depends upon it maintaining overwhelming military power. We have all become so fixated on looking for what has altered since 1989 that we sometimes fail to see what has not.[1]

Summary of findings

The domestic setting

It is impossible to make sense of US foreign policy without taking serious account of the American domestic setting. Chapter 2 confirmed that US foreign policy does not 'stop at the water's edge'. Now more than ever in an age of geo-economics and Congressional self-confidence, the dividing line between the domestic and the foreign has become even more blurred. In addition, because of the fall of the USSR and the accompanying decline of US presidential power (the age of the Imperial President has passed for good), policy-makers are finding it more and more difficult to mobilize popular consent for bold and decisive action in the international arena. Thus rhetorical calls by critics for the White House to provide stronger leadership and be more decisive abroad ignore the objective constraints which make it extremely difficult for any president to lead in a post-communist environment.

Critics of American indecision also appear to ignore another, equally uncomfortable fact: that presidents who have tried to provide leadership abroad have not always been very popular at home. Americans, we should recall, were not noticeably enthusiastic about going to war with Iraq in 1991. They have shown little inclination for direct military involvement in Bosnia. They were even unsettled when Clinton sent troops to liberate Haiti against a non-existent opposition. Bold calls for the United States to lead are thus almost futile if the populace itself refuses to be led. Facing multiple problems at home in a situation where there is no clear and present danger to the national interest, Americans have simply not been prepared to support the deployment of US forces overseas. This does not make them isolationist in the classic sense. As Ronald Steel has observed, there is no serious support for such a posture in the United States today.[2] On the other hand, it does make them very cautious – and somewhat more selfish and self-interested as well, as the Republican landslide in November 1994 clearly indicated.

Economics

As Jim Hoagland has pointed out, 'America's foreign policy is about more than just trade'. It is also true, as was pointed out at the end of

Chapter 3, that Clinton's political economy contains important contradictions. Nevertheless, there really has been a major sea-change here, perhaps just as important as the conceptual revolution that occurred between 1945 and 1950 and that laid the intellectual foundations for the Cold War.[3] Certain conclusions follow from this. One, most obviously, is that the United States will tend to view old friends in increasingly competitive terms, as Japan and the European Union have already discovered to their cost. Another is that although this geo-economic drive will not necessarily lead to trade wars in the classical sense, it could weaken (and probably already has) the bonds holding the key democracies together. There is also little reason to think that the situation will change, even if Clinton were to be replaced by a Republican. In effect, the United States seems set on an economic course – to maximize trade share, to open up closed markets, and to make itself more competitive – which will command popular support at home even if (and perhaps because) it irritates and annoys traditional allies abroad.

Defence

Although spending on defence will continue to fall, military questions still have the capacity to generate controversy. One might have predicted otherwise given the collapse of the USSR and the evident desire on the part of most Americans to cut the military budget as a way of reducing the US deficit. However, as the analysis in Chapter 4 has shown, there are powerful factors – both internal and global – that will ensure that the issue of US military strength will remain high on the American political agenda. Moreover, on military matters Clinton has proved to be remarkably hard-nosed; in fact, in this area, there is not a great deal to distinguish his policies from those of his Republican predecessor. The real problem perhaps is not whether Clinton has turned out to be too weak on defence, but whether or not the United States can actually afford to pay for the forces deemed to be necessary to fight and win two regional wars simultaneously. In the meantime, it can at least feel reassured by the fact that at no time over the past half century has it ever been so secure militarily.

Relations with Russia

Dealing with post-communist Russia has proved to be, and will almost certainly remain, a most difficult job – not because Moscow is likely to seek confrontation with the West, but rather because the future of Russia is unclear, the success of the reform process uncertain, and Russia's national interests by no means the same as those of the United States. For these reasons, talk of a grand alliance or partnership with Russian reform has proved to be premature. Nevertheless, as Chapter 5 has shown, Russia is simply too important to be left out in the cold; and whoever occupies the White House or controls Congress in the future will have to find ways of cooperating with Moscow. This will not yield a great deal of economic fruit. On the other hand, the political and military arguments for working with America's former adversary are so overwhelming that they will almost certainly outweigh any other pressures pushing the United States back towards some new form of containment.

Europe and the Pacific Rim

Since 1989 the United States has been forced to find new means of relating to both Europe and the Pacific Rim – two regions it considers far too important to be neglected, but much more difficult to manage now that neither is threatened by the USSR. Significantly, though, in spite of all the grand American rhetoric since 1993 about the unparalleled importance of the Asia-Pacific region, the analysis in Chapters 6 and 7 suggests that the United States continues to find it much easier to relate to the nations across the Atlantic than those on the other side of the Pacific. Although the transatlantic relationship has not been without its difficulties since 1989 – most vividly illustrated in policy clashes over former Yugoslavia – these are almost insignificant compared with the problems the United States experienced with many of the countries along the Pacific Rim. In the light of this, current US assumptions about the creation of an integrated Pacific community may well turn out to be far too optimistic. By the same token, predictions about the souring of relations between the United States and Europe could prove to be much too pessimistic.

The 'Third World'

The 'Third World', once viewed and treated as a relatively homogeneous entity during the Cold War, is now, as Chapter 8 makes clear, a complex series of regions with different problems and specific requirements. Here it is almost impossible now to talk of a single US strategy; there is, rather, a series of policies all designed to achieve the same goals of democratic consolidation, market-led development and closer integration of the developing countries into the world market. In spite of the collapse of communism, the United States cannot afford to ignore what happens in the Third World: partly because many of the less developed countries will one day be far more significant economically, but more importantly because the most obvious sources of international instability today (and for the foreseeable future) will be the tensions and conflicts arising from contradictions on the so-called periphery.

The future of US foreign policy

But what of the tests facing the United States as it moves towards the 1996 election and beyond towards the new millennium? There is little point in restating what others have already implored the United States to do or not to do abroad. Nor is it the job of an analyst to advise governments or states on how best to advance their own interests. But one observation is in order, and can perhaps be best posed in the form of a question: what price is the United States actually prepared to pay to build a new, and possibly better, world order? As we have suggested, those who invoke the United States to act with greater determination ignore the objective obstacles preventing it from doing so. But there is a world of difference between avoiding unnecessary entanglements in conflicts where there is no vital US interest at stake and rejecting serious engagement altogether. And it does seem to many observers that by opting for what looks like the safer and cheaper course of action – in reality refusing to take the risks or pay the cost involved in being a superpower – the United States may be surrendering a golden opportunity. Nearly all observers are agreed that without the US there can be no world order. But as long as the United States remains a reluctant superpower the chances of that order being constructed in the wake of the Cold War are likely to remain remote.[4]

Notes

The following abbreviations have been used throughout the notes:

FA *Foreign Affairs*
FT *The Financial Times*
IHT *International Herald Tribune*
NYT *New York Times*

Chapter 1: Introduction

1 George F. Kennan, *Around the Cragged Hill: A Personal and Political Philosophy* (New York, W.W. Norton, 1993), p. 180.
2 See Norman Ornstein, 'Foreign Policy and the 1992 Elections', *FA*, vol. 71, no. 3, Summer 1992, pp. 1–16.
3 See Henry Kissinger, 'At Sea in a New World', *Newsweek*, 6 June 1994, pp. 6–8.
4 See Tony Smith, *America's Mission: The United States and the Worldwide Struggle for Democracy in the Twentieth Century* (Princeton, New Jersey, Princeton University Press, 1994).
5 See Laurence Martin, 'The Changing Role Of The US In Global Order', in Seizaburo Sato and Trevor Taylor, eds, *Prospects For Global Order* (London, Royal Institute of International Affairs, 1993), p. 85.
6 See, for example, Jurek Martin, 'Clinton explains what in the world he is doing', *FT*, 5 May 1994; 'A little late to be waking up, *Economist*, 21 May 1994; Jim Hoagland, 'His Foreign Policy Just Keeps Drifting', *IHT*, 31 May 1994; and Martin Ivens, 'A statesman looks at the new world chaos', *The Times*, 1 June 1994.
7 See Raymond Seitz, 'From the jaws of victory', *Economist*, 27 May 1995, pp. 23–5.

8 See 'Why America doesn't lead', *Economist*, 30 April 1994.
9 See Michael Cox, 'American power and the Soviet threat: US foreign policy and the Cold War', in Anthony McGrew, ed., *The United States in The Twentieth Century: Empire* (London, Hodder and Stoughton, 1994), pp. 19–66.

Chapter 2: The constrained superpower?

1 Richard Maidment and Anthony McGrew, *The American Political Process* (London, Sage Publications, 1991), p. 139.
2 I.M. Destler, Leslie Gelb and Anthony Lake, *Our Own Worst Enemy: The Unmaking of American Foreign Policy* (New York, Simon and Schuster, 1984).
3 George F. Kennan, *Around the Cragged Hill: A Personal and Political Philosophy* (New York, W. W. Norton, 1993), esp. pp. 17–36.
4 Edward S. Corwin, *The President: Office and Powers* (New York, New York University Press, 1940), p. 200.
5 Michael Foley, 'Congress and policy-making: can it cope with foreign affairs?', in Robert Williams, ed., *Explaining American Politics: Issues and Interpretations* (London, Routledge, 1990), p. 65.
6 John Dumbrell, *The Making of US Foreign Policy* (Manchester University Press, 1990), p. 91.
7 Foley, p. 66; Dumbrell, p. 91.
8 Koichi Suzuki, L. Alexander Norsworthy and Helen C. Gleason, *The Clinton Revolution: An Inside Look at the New Administration* (Lanham, University Press of America, 1993), pp. 3–4.
9 The central theme of the Clinton presidential campaign was (as he put it himself) that if the United States was not 'strong at home' it would inevitably be 'weaker abroad'. See his speech given to North Carolina State University on 4 October 1992. Cited in *Clinton On Foreign Policy Issues* (London, United States Information Service, n.d.), p. 9.
10 All administrations, of course, have been sensitive to public opinion. It is significant, however, that the first truly post-Cold War administration was especially sensitive. This was made very clear to me in an interview I conducted in February 1993 with a staff member working in the White House. After a comprehensive review of Clinton's foreign policy, the official spent a considerable time discussing a poll which had been conducted for the *Los Angeles Times* the previous year. The poll showed that Americans were no longer concerned about classic security issues, and were interested in the outside world only to the degree that the outside world impinged on their lives in the shape of, say, imported drugs or illegal immigrants. The official made it quite clear that polls in general (and possibly this poll in particular) played a large part in the way the

Clinton administration thought about foreign policy. Indeed, the best foreign policy, in his view, was one which did not make the front pages of the next morning's newspapers.

11 My reading of US foreign policy after the Cold War runs in quite the opposite direction, therefore, to that suggested by Robert W. Tucker and David C. Hendrickson in *The Imperial Temptation: the New World Order and America's Purpose* (New York, Council on Foreign Relations Press, 1992).

12 See Peter W. Rodman, 'Bill's World', *National Review*, 15 November 1993, pp. 34–40.

13 See James M. Lindsey, 'Congress and Foreign Policy: Why the Hill Matters', *Political Science Quarterly*, vol. 107, no. 4, 1992–3, pp. 607–28.

14 John Isaacs, 'Right turn ahead', *Bulletin of the Atomic Scientists*, vol. 51, no. 1, January–February 1995, p. 16.

15 The Republicans won eight Senate seats previously held by Democrats, then picked up a ninth when Richard Shelby of Alabama switched partisan allegiance. As a result the Republicans now had 53 seats and the Democrats 47 in the Senate. Over 60 seats changed hands in the House elections, giving the Republicans 230 seats to the Democrats' 204. For an excellent analysis, see Douglas W. Jaenicke, 'The 1994 United States Congressional Elections: An Electoral Earthquake, Tremor or Both?', Paper delivered at the Annual Meeting of the American Politics Group of the Political Studies Association of the UK, University of Keele, 4–6 January 1995.

16 For a highly critical assessment of the Republican programme, see James Fallows, 'The Republican Promise', *New York Review of Books*, 12 January 1995, pp. 3–6.

17 See Newt Gingrich, 'Gingrich Looks Ahead', *IHT*, 23 February 1995.

18 See *Contract With America* (Washington, House Republican Conference, 1994).

19 Isaacs, p. 16.

20 The 'National Revitalization Act' went forward on 4 January 1995. It was divided into seven parts. Part I was a general preamble under the heading of Findings, Policy and Purposes. Part II discussed Missile Defense; Part III the Revitalization of National Security Commission; Part IV Command of United States Forces; Part V United Nations; Part VI Revitalization and Expansion of the North Atlantic Treaty Organization; and Part VII Budget Firewalls.

21 See Warren Christopher and William J. Perry, 'A Bill to Maim American Foreign Policy', *IHT*, 14 February 1995.

22 Richard Cohen, 'A Familiar Mood in America, and Again It's Wrong', *IHT*, 22 February 1995.

23 A 1994 study published by the Program on International Policy Attitudes, School of Public Affairs, University of Maryland showed that 75 per cent of Americans felt that the country was spending 'too much' on foreign aid. Those polled, however, overestimated to a huge degree what was actually being spent on aid – the median guess being around 15 per cent of the American budget!

24 See Thomas L. Friedman, 'The Drive-By Republicans Take a Cheap Shot at the Peacekeepers', *IHT*, 20 February 1995.

25 A point well observed by Martin Walker in 'Clinton rolls back aid and defence', *Guardian*, 8 February 1994.

26 On the struggle to save AID, USIA and ACDA, see Steven Greenhouse, 'Gore Rules Against Merger of A.I.D. and Others Into State Dept.', *NYT*, 26 January 1995; and Thomas L. Lippman, 'Gore Is Said to Reject Merger of Foreign Policy Agencies', *Washington Post*, 26 January 1995.

27 According to one analyst, the NEC under Robert Rubin probably had more influence over the Clinton administration's direction than any other body. See John B. Judis, 'Old Master', *New Republic*, 13 December 1993, pp. 24–8.

28 Walter Pincus, 'CIA Waits Anxiously for New Chief', *Washington Post*, 24 January 1995.

29 Quote from Tim Weiner, 'Congress Decides To Conduct Study Of Need For C.I.A.', *NYT*, 28 September 1994.

30 One significant change that had already taken place (or was being discussed) at the CIA, and within other intelligence agencies, was the delicate issue of whether or not to use their services to advance US economic goals. Senator DeConcini, Chairman of the Select Committee on Intelligence – which began to examine what Director Woolsey called this 'hottest' of topics back in 1991 – provided perhaps the definitive public exposition on the subject. In his view, though the intelligence community should 'not attempt to satisfy' private firms directly, it could help them indirectly and thus 'assist the international competitiveness of domestic industry' by passing on information to 'departments or agencies' of government such as the newly created National Economic Committee, the Office of the US Trade Representatives, and the Departments of State and Commerce. He concluded that 'while the role of the intelligence community is limited, we should utilize its capabilities where appropriate to promote and protect the interests of the United States'. See Senator Dennis DeConcini, 'The Role of U.S. Intelligence in Promoting Economic Interests', *Journal of International Affairs*, vol. 48, no. 1, Summer 1994, pp. 39–58.

31 Sidney Blumenthal, 'The Return of the Repressed: Anti-Internationalism and the American Right', Paper presented to the Conference on 'Kennan, the Cold War, and the Future of American Foreign Policy', School of International Relations, University of Southern California, 27–29 January 1995.

32 Al Richman, 'The American Public's "Rules Of Military Engagement" In The Post Cold War Era', Paper presented to the American Political Science Association, New York City, 2 September 1994.

33 I have drawn my evidence here from three memoranda made available to me by the United States Information Agency in Washington DC: *Amplifications of Findings on Internationalism/Isolationism in the U.S.*, 19 January 1994; *American Public's Views on GATT and U.S. World Role*, 28 November 1994; and *Times Mirror Shows Most Americans Continue to Back NATO*, 13 December 1994.

34 One official remarked to me in February 1994 that if Bush had become president, the USA might have become more isolationist. But because of his 'laser-like' focus on the imperative need for the United States to compete in world markets, Clinton had been able to attack isolationism more effectively.

Chapter 3: From geopolitics to geo-economics?

1 See Micky Kantor, *US Trade Policy and the Post-Cold War World*, Statement before the Senate Finance Committee, Washington DC, 9 March 1993 (US Department of State Dispatch, 15 March 1993, vol. 4, no. 11), p. 144.

2 See Lester Thurrow, *Head to Head: The Coming Economic Battle among Japan, Europe, and America* (New York, William Morrow and Company Inc. 1992), pp. 14–17.

3 See Michael Borrus, Steve Weber, and John Zysman with Joseph Willihnganz, 'Mercantilism and Global Security', *The National Interest*, Fall 1992, pp. 21–9.

4 See Jeffrey E. Garten, 'Challenges of the Global Marketplace: If You Don't Win, You Lose', presentation to the Royal Institute of International Affairs, London, 11 July 1995.

5 Martin Fletcher, 'Rough diamond Clinton cuts tough deals on trade', *The Times*, 15 February 1994.

6 Quote from Jeffrey E. Garten speech, 'The Clinton Administration's Trade Priorities for 1994 ... and Reflections on Europe', *Atlantic Outlook*, 28 January 1994, pp. 1–2.

7 See *Clinton On Foreign Policy Issues*, The Reference Center, United States Information Service, Embassy of the United States of America, London, 1992.

8 For Jeffrey Garten's views see his article 'Clinton's Emerging Trade Policy', *FA*, vol. 72, no. 3, Summer 1993, pp. 182–9.

9 Peter F. Cowhey, Jonathan D. Aronson, 'A New Trade Order', *FA*, vol. 72, no. 1, 1993, pp. 183–95.

10 See Martin Walker, 'The End of the Imperial Presidency', Paper presented

to the School of International Relations, Center of International Studies of the University of California, Conference on 'Kennan, the Cold War, and the Future of American Foreign Policy', 27–29 January 1995.

11 On Tyson's views on trade see also Rudiger W. Dornbusch, Anne O. Krueger and Laura D'Andrea Tyson, *An American Trade Strategy: Options for the 1990s* (The Brookings Institution, Washington DC, 1990).

12 See also Jeffrey E. Garten, 'Clinton's Emerging Trade Policy: Act One, Scene One', *FA*, vol. 72, no. 3, Summer 1993, pp. 182–9.

13 For a brief guide to Theodore Moran's economic thinking see his article, 'An Economics Agenda for Neorealists', *International Security*, vol. 18, no. 2, 1993, pp. 211–15.

14 See Ira C. Magaziner and Robert B. Reich, *Minding America's Business: the Decline and Rise of the American Economy* (New York, Vintage Books, 1983) and Robert B. Reich, *The Next American Frontier: A Provocative Program for Economic Renewal* (New York, Penguin Books, 1984).

15 Robert B. Reich, *The Work of Nations* (New York, Vintage, 1992).

16 James Adams, 'Business swings behind Clinton', *Sunday Times*, 25 October 1992.

17 Leonard Silk, 'Head Off A Trade War', *NYT*, 4 February 1993.

18 See Michael Prowse, 'A Prussian in the White House', *FT*, 21 February 1994.

19 Adrian Hamilton, 'A whiff of US imperialism', *Observer*, 12 December 1993.

20 Paul Krugman, 'Competitiveness: A Dangerous Obsession', *FA*, vol. 73, no. 2, March–April 1994, pp. 28–44.

21 See Nora Lustig, Barry P. Bosworth and Robert Z. Lawrence, eds., *North American Free Trade: Assessing the Impact* (The Brookings Institution, Washington DC, 1992).

22 See Micky Kantor, 'Regional Arrangements Facilitate Global Trade', *Atlantic Outlook*, 22 October 1993, pp. 1–2.

23 See David E. Sanger, 'Clinton In Seattle For Pacific Talks To Seek Markets', *NYT*, 19 November 1994; Roger Cohen, 'Like the U.S., Western Europe Steps Up Its Trade With Asia', *NYT*, 24 November 1993.

24 See 'GATT Deal', *Daily Telegraph*, 15 December 1993.

25 Figures about world trade after GATT from Martin Wolf, 'Doing good, despite themselves', *FT*, 16 December 1993.

26 Nancy Dunne, 'A round sceptic seeking a square deal', *FT*, 2 December 1993.

27 See *Towards a National Export Strategy*. Report to the United States Congress (Washington DC, 30 September 1993). The importance of the report in creating America's first national export strategy was emphasized in Clinton's national security reviews. See, for example, *A National Security Strategy Of Engagement And Enlargement* (The White House, February 1995), p. 19.

28 Jurek Martin and Nancy Dunne, 'Turning the moribund into mainstream', *FT*, 21 February 1994.
29 See Don E. Kash and Robert W. Rycroft, 'Nurturing Winners with Federal R&D', *Technology Review*, November–December 1993, pp. 58–64.
30 Deborah Shapley, 'Clintonizing Science Policy', *The Bulletin of the Atomic Scientists*, December 1993, pp. 39–43.
31 On the Saudi deal see Thomas L. Friedman, 'Saudi Air To Buy $6bn In Jets Built In the U.S.', *NYT*, 17 February 1994.
32 Garten, 'Challenges of the Global Marketplace'.
33 Manuel Saragosa, 'US pressure on trade deals in Asia pays off', *FT*, 17 November 1994.
34 Nancy Dunne and Michael Cassell, 'Big brother lends a hand', *FT*, 15 February 1995.

Chapter 4: Planning for the next war

1 Inis L. Claude, *Swords into Plowshares: The Problems and Progress of International Organizations* (New York, Random House, 1956).
2 See Walter Millis, ed., *The Forrestal Diaries* (London, Cassell, 1951), p. 336.
3 On the transition to military containment see Michael Cox, 'Requiem for a Cold War Critic – George F. Kennan: 1946–1950', *Irish Slavonic Studies*, No. 11, 1990–1991, pp. 1–35.
4 See *Foreign Relations of the United States 1950, Volume I* (USGPO, Washington DC, 1977), pp. 290–91.
5 On Reagan and Russia see Michael Cox, 'Whatever Happened to the "Second" Cold War? Soviet–American Relations: 1980–1988', *Review of International Studies*, vol. 16, no. 2, April 1990, pp. 155–72.
6 See 'Aspin Spells Out Further Proposed Cuts In U.S. Military', London, United States Information Service, 3 September 1993.
7 Though according to Colin Powell, the Bush presidency actually 'anticipated' and presumably planned for the collapse of the USSR! See his comments in *Threat Assessment, Military Strategy, and Defense Planning*, Hearings Before The Committee On Armed Services, United States Senate (USGPO, Washington DC, 1992), p. 460.
8 See the excellent analysis provided by Colin McInnes in his 'From the Bottom Up? Conventional Forces and Defence Policy after the Cold War', *Contemporary Security Policy*, vol. 15, no. 3, December 1994, pp. 147–69.
9 On Bush's initial hesitancy over nuclear arms control see the definitive analysis by Steve Smith, 'The Superpowers and Arms Control in the Era of the "Second Cold War"', in Michael Cox, ed., *Beyond the Cold War: Superpowers at the Crossroads?* (Lanham, University Press of America, 1990), pp. 167–84. On START see Michael Cox, 'From Superpower

Detente to Entente Cordiale? Soviet–US Relations: 1989–90', in Bruce George, ed., *Jane's Nato Handbook, 1990–91* (Surrey, Jane's Information Group, 1990), pp. 277–86.

10 See Leslie Gelb, '$1.5 Trillion "Defense"', *NYT*, 17 April 1992.

11 See Dick Cheney in *Soviet Military Power: 1990* (USGPO, Washington DC, September 1990), pp. 3–5.

12 Though even after the fall of the USSR, Robert Gates, Director of the CIA, was still urging military caution on the United States. See his testimony in *Threat Assessment, Military Strategy, and Defense Planning*, pp. 16–18.

13 See *National Security Strategy of the United States* (USGPO, Washington DC, 1993), p. 1.

14 See David Stockman, *The Triumph of Politics* (London, Hodder and Stoughton, 1987), p. 136.

15 See the important speech on defence policy made by Les Aspin to the Atlantic Council on 6 January 1992, reprinted as 'Aspin To Look At Changes In U.S. Military Posture'.

16 See Les Aspin, Secretary of Defense, *The Bottom-Up Review: Forces For A New Era*, 1 September 1993, pp. 10–11.

17 Figures on Clinton's defence budget can be found in *FY 1995 Defense Budget*, Office of Assistant Secretary of Defense (Washington DC, 7 February 1994).

18 See Colin Gray, *Off The Map: Defense Planning After The Soviet Threat*, Paper presented to British International Studies Association, University of Warwick, 15 December 1993.

19 See Dov S. Zakheim, 'A New Name for Winning: Losing', *NYT*, 19 June 1993.

20 See 'Two Wars, One Budget', *IHT*, 16 September 1994.

21 Colin McInnes, p. 164.

22 Andrew F. Krepinevich, Jr. 'The Clinton Defense Program: Assessing The Bottom-Up Review', *Strategic Review*, Spring 1994, pp. 19–20.

23 Rober L. Borosage, 'Inventing the Threat: Clinton's Defense Budget', *World Policy Journal*, vol. X, no. 4, Winter 1993/4, pp. 7–15.

24 For the best guide to the issue see Zachary S. Davis, *U.S. Counterproliferation Doctrine: Issues for Congress*, Congressional Research Service, The Library of Congress (Washington DC, 21 September 1994).

25 See Leonard S. Spector, 'Neo-Nonproliferation', *Survival*, vol. 37, no. 1, Spring 1995, pp. 66–85.

26 See *U.S. Nonproliferation Policy*, Hearing Before The Committee On Foreign Affairs, House Of Representatives (USGPO, Washington DC, 10 November 1993), and Council On Foreign Relations Memorandum, *Final Report of the Task Force on Nonproliferation*, 12 January 1995, 30pp.

27 For background on how the United States got the NPT passed in April 1995 see Julia Preston and R. Jeffrey Smith, 'A Concerted Effort Brings Treaty Coup', *IHT*, 15 May 1995, and Julian Ozanne, 'Gore asks for Arab support over N-treaty', *FT*, 24 March 1995.
28 See Michael Littlejohns and Bernard Gray, 'N-weapons treaty made permanent', *FT*, 12 May 1995, and Zachary S. Davis, 'Nuclear Proliferation and the Future of the Non-Proliferation Treaty: Coping with Best and Worst Cases', *Irish Studies in International Affairs*, vol. 6, 1995.
29 Michael Wines, 'Aspin Orders Pentagon Overhaul Of Strategy on Nuclear Weapons', *NYT*, 30 September 1993.
30 Quoted in Robert A. Manning, 'Ending The Nuclear Century', *The New Democrat*, January/February 1995, p. 55.
31 'Remarks Prepared For Delivery By Secretary Of Defense William J. Perry To The Henry L. Stimson Center' (Office Of Assistant Secretary Of Defense, Washington DC), 20 September 1994.
32 For a stimulating analysis of the problem, see Robert A. Manning, *Back to the Future: Toward a Post-Nuclear Ethic – The New Logic of Nonproliferation* (Progressive Foundation, Washington DC), January 1994.
33 For a brilliant discussion of America's possible 'national identity' crisis in a post-Soviet world see Robert B. Reich, *The Work Of Nations* (New York, Vintage Books, 1992), pp. 317–24.

Chapter 5: Strategic alliance or cold peace?

1 Stroke Talbott, *US Department of State Dispatch*, vol. 5, no. 5, 31 January 1994.
2 Quoted in *The Future of U.S. Foreign Policy in the Post-Cold War Era* (USGPO, Washington DC, 1992), p. 8.
3 See *Clinton on Foreign Policy Issues* (London, United States Information Service, n.d.), pp. 22, 35, 45.
4 Strobe Talbott, 'Post-Victory Blues', *FA*, vol. 71, no. 1, 1992, pp. 53–69.
5 See Clinton's comments on aid to Russia in *American Leadership and Global Change* (US Department of State Dispatch), 1 March 1993, vol. 4, no. 9, p. 118.
6 See also *The Future of U.S. Foreign Policy (Part I): Regional Issues* (USGPO, Washington DC, 1993), pp. 396–416, 453–79.
7 See Secretary Christopher, *Securing US Interests While Supporting Russian Reform* (US Department of State Dispatch), 29 March 1993, vol. 4, no. 13.
8 On Clinton's Russian strategy see Strobe Talbott, *US Must Lead a Strategic Alliance With Post-Soviet Reform* (US Department of State Dispatch), 26 April 1993, vol. 4. no. 17; President Clinton, *A Strategic Alliance With Russian Reform* (US Department of State Dispatch), 5 April

1993, vol. 4, no. 14; and his *New Democratic Partnership Between The United States and Russia* (US Department of State Dispatch), 12 April 1993, vol. 4, no. 15.

9 See *Focus on Russia: Highlights of Successful U. S. Support for Market Reform* (US Department of State Dispatch), 3 January 1994, vol. 5, no. 1, p. 3.

10 See Michael Mandelbaum and Strobe Talbott, *At the Highest Level: the Inside Story of the end of the Cold War* (London, Warner Books, 1994), p. 472.

11 See Secretary Christopher, *Securing US Interests While Securing Russian Reform,* p. 175.

12 See Kurt C. Campbell et al., *Soviet Nuclear Fission: Control of the Nuclear Arsenal in a Disintegrating Soviet Union* (Harvard University, CSIA Studies in International Security, No. 1, 1 November 1991).

13 See *U.S. Nonproliferation Policy* (USGPO, Washington DC, 1994).

14 See *Threat Assessment, Military Strategy, and Defense Planning* (USGPO, Washington DC, 1992), pp. 17–18.

15 See Martin Walker, 'Make or break for Big Daddy', *Guardian*, 7 January 1994.

16 See Martin Fletcher, 'Bush says Clinton has hurt image of US leadership', *The Times*, 29 January 1994.

17 See Peter Reddaway, 'Visit to a Maelstrom', *NYT*, 10 January 1994.

18 See Jonathan Steele, 'The bear's necessities', *Guardian*, 4 January 1993; Serge Schemann, 'Yeltsin critical of U.S. role in Balkans and Iraq', *NYT*, 26 January 1993; 'Old Thinking', *FT*, 20 January 1994; and Sergei Karaganov, 'Russia finds independent foreign policy', *FT*, 21 March 1994.

19 See Douglas Hurd and Andrei Kozyrev, 'Challenge of peacekeeping', *FT*, 14 December 1993.

20 See Jonathan Eyal, 'This affair will end in tears', *Independent*, 13 January 1994.

21 On Russian opposition to NATO expansion see Andranik Migranyan, 'Partnership for Peace: No, Russia is too big for this exercise', *IHT*, 24 June 1994; Bruce Clark, 'Old enemies make tricky friends', *FT*, 9 June 1994; and Stephen Rosenfeld, 'A Russian makes a case against NATO expansion', *IHT*, 8 July 1994.

22 Elaine Sciolino, 'Clinton Reaffirms Policy on Yeltsin', *NYT*, 16 December 1993.

23 R. W. Apple, 'Results in Russia shake Washington', *NYT*, 15 December 1993.

24 Martin Fletcher, 'Yeltsin gives America assurance on reforms', *The Times*, 16 December 1993.

25 Elaine Sciolino, 'U.S. is abandoning "Shock Therapy" for the Russians', *NYT*, 21 December 1993.

26 George Graham, 'IMF–World Bank warning on Russia', *FT*, 7 January 1994.
27 See Steven Erlanger, '2 Western Economists Quit Russia Posts', *NYT*, 22 January 1994.
28 Peter Passell, 'Russia's political turmoil follows half steps, not shock therapy', *NYT*, 30 December 1993. See also 'Reforming Russia's Economy', *Economist*, 11 December 1993, pp. 27–9.
29 Peter Reddaway, 'Russia's sun sets in the West', *Independent*, 24 February 1994.
30 See Martin Fletcher and Anne McElvoy, 'Clinton goes on TV sales pitch for Yeltsin reforms', *The Times*, 15 January 1994.
31 Strobe Talbott, *America Must Remain Engaged in Russian Reform* (US Department of State Dispatch), 31 January 1994, vol. 5, no. 5.
32 For a critique of Talbott see William Safire, 'Kozyrev and Talbott', *NYT*, 27 January 1994.
33 Strobe Talbott, *America Must Remain Engaged in Russian Reform.*
34 'The Spy Case: The Fallout', *Washington Post*, 25 February 1994.
35 Charles Krauthammer, 'Honeymoon over, the two powers go their own way', *IHT*, 26 February 1994.
36 Quoted in Martin Walker, 'Major to temper Clinton's "new realism" over Russia', *Guardian*, 1 March 1994.
37 See *Confirmation Statement for Strobe Talbott as Deputy Secretary of State: Senate Foreign Relations Committee*, 8 February 1994.
38 Helen Dewar, 'Senate backs Talbott for State Department', *Washington Post*, 23 February 1994.
39 Zbigniew Brzezinski, 'The Premature Partnership', *FA*, March–April 1994, vol. 73, no. 2, pp. 67–82.
40 'A tale of two bears', *Economist*, 12 March 1994, p. 60.
41 See also Zbigniew Brzezinski, 'A bigger – and – safer Europe', *NYT*, 1 December 1993.
42 For a critique of Brzezinski see Stephen Sestanovich, 'Giving Russia its Due', *The National Interest*, Summer 1994, pp. 3–13.
43 Strobe Talbott, *America Must Remain Engaged in Russian Reform*, p. 40.
44 See Zbigniew Brzezinski, 'Improved U.S. policy for Russia and Central Europe', *IHT*, 29 June 1994.
45 Michael R. Gordon, 'Perry says caution is vital to Russian partnership', *NYT*, 15 March 1994. Following a meeting in Vladivostok between Warren Christopher and Andrei Kozyrev, Christopher stated that 'we recognize that as large nations with large interests we are bound to have differences, but we pledge to deal with our differences openly'. Quoted in *FT*, 15 March 1994.
46 John Lloyd, 'IMF gives go-ahead for $1.5bn loan to Russia', *FT*, 23 March 1994, and 'Moscow's monetarist swerve wins over IMF', *FT*, 24 March 1994.

47 Title of interview conducted with Prime Minister Viktor Chernomyrdin in the *Financial Times*, 16 May 1994.
48 Tom Buerkle, 'Trade accord widens Russian access to EU', *IHT*, 12 May 1994, and Charles Goldsmith, 'Yeltsin arrives at summit to sign key accord with EU', *Wall Street Journal*, 24 June 1994.
49 Ian Black, 'Russia's marriage to West on a rocky road', *Guardian*, 24 June 1994.
50 Daniel Williams, 'Russia signs on with NATO in peace alliance', *IHT*, 23 June 1994, and Mark Frankland, 'Russia rogue elephant slips into Nato camp', *Observer*, 26 June 1994.
51 See Andrei Kozyrev, 'The Lagging Partnershp', *FA*, May – June 1994, Vol. 73. No. 3, pp. 59–71, and his 'You can't expect angels to appear overnight', *Time*, 11 July 1994, p. 34.
52 See Jonathan Eyal, 'More a nadir than a summit', *Independent*, 7 July 1994.
53 See Jim Hoagland, 'Clinton and Yeltsin Had Better Make Up in Moscow', *IHT*, 4 May 1995.
54 See Frances Williams, 'US–Russian "honeymoon is over"', *FT*, 24 March 1995.
55 See Michael Dobbs and R. Jeffrey Smith, 'Summit Accord Over Security Is Taking Shape', and Margaret Shapiro and R. Jeffrey Smith, 'Russia Is Seen to Bend on Key Nuclear System', *IHT*, 8 May 1995.

Chapter 6: Atlantic rift?

1 Quoted in Thomas H. Etzold and John L. Gaddis, eds, *Containment: Documents On American Policy And Strategy, 1945–1950* (New York, Columbia University Press, 1978), pp. 108–9.
2 See Stanley Sloan, 'Transatlantic relations in the wake of the Brussels Summit', *NATO Review*, vol. 42, no. 2, April 1994, p. 27.
3 See Geir Lundestad, *The American 'Empire'* (Oxford University Press, 1990).
4 See Anton Deporte, *Europe Between The Superpowers* (New Haven, Yale University Press, 1978).
5 Quote from NSC 58 (1949), cited in Etzold and Gaddis, p. 223.
6 Allen Lynch, *The Cold War Is Over – Again* (Boulder, Westview Press, 1992), pp. 2–3.
7 See Michael Smith and Stephen Woolcock, *The United States and the European Community in a Transformed World* (London, Pinter/Royal Institute of International Affairs, 1993), p. 1.
8 See Richard Nixon, 'Is America a Part Of Europe?', *National Review*, 2 March 1992, pp. 26–31.
9 For the definitive guide to the US response to a changing European

Community see *1992: The Effects of Greater European Economic Integration Within the European Community on the United States* (Washington DC, United States International Trade Commission, 1990–1993, 5 vols.).

10 See J.M.C. Rollo et al., *The New Eastern Europe: Western Responses* (London, Pinter/Royal Institute of International Affairs, 1990).

11 On Germany in the new Europe see Barbara Lippert and Rosalind Stevens-Ströhmann, *German Unification and EC Integration: German and British Perspectives* (London, Pinter/Royal Institute of International Affairs, 1993).

12 All quotes from Secretary Baker, *A New Europe, A New Atlanticism: Architecture for a New Era*, Current Policy No. 1233 (Washington DC, United States Department of State), 12 December 1989.

13 Harold Brown, 'Europe: A Sound U.S. Policy of Initiative and Insurance', *IHT*, 27 August 1994.

14 Strobe Talbott, 'Post-victory blues', *FA*, vol. 71, no. 1, 1992, pp. 53–69.

15 On US views about European integration see Glennon J. Harrison, ed., *Europe and the United States: Competition and Cooperation in the 1990s* (New York, M. E. Sharpe, 1994); and James B. Steinberg, *'An Ever Closer Union': European Integration and its Implications for the Future of U.S. – European Relations* (Santa Monica, RAND, 1993).

16 See Hugh Miall, *Shaping the New Europe* (London, Pinter/Royal Institute of International Affairs, 1993).

17 Michael Evans, 'Birth of Euro-army spurs Nato unease', *The Times*, 21 May 1992.

18 Quote from a Bush official in James Adams, 'Rebel allies flex muscles as Britain tries to save Nato', *Sunday Times*, 10 May 1992.

19 See Hella Pick, 'Appeals to abandon plans for Franco-German corps ignored', *Guardian*, 7 April 1992.

20 See *Economist*, 19 February 1994, pp. 19–24.

21 Jurek Martin, 'Heart in Europe, hopes on Asia', *FT*, 24 November 1993.

22 See Stanley Sloan, *NATO Review*, pp. 27–28.

23 See Richard Holbrooke, Assistant Secretary of State for European and Canadian Affairs, *'U.S. Works to Build New European Security Architecture'*, 3 March 1994, Testimony before the Senate Appropriations Subcommittee on Foreign Operations.

24 See the comments by Ambassador Stuart Eizenstat, the US representative to the European Union in 'The United States Backs the Process of European Integration', *IHT*, 19 August 1994.

25 Stanley Sloan, *NATO Review*, p. 29.

26 Figures quoted by Stephen A. Oxman, Assistant Secretary of State for European and Canadian Affairs in 'Partnership with Europe is the Best U.S. Hope for the Future', speech made to the National Foreign Policy

Conference for Leaders in Higher Education at the Department of State, 18 April 1994.

27 See *The Times* editorial, 22 December 1993.

28 See Jim Hoagland, 'Cold Spell: Ulster and the Balkans Come Between Clinton and Major', *IHT*, 16 March 1995.

29 Edward Mortimer, 'In search of an enemy', *FT*, 7 December 1994.

30 See Richard Holbrooke, 'America, A European Power', *FA*, vol. 74, no. 2, March–April 1995.

31 See Paul E. Gallis, *Partnership For Peace* (Washington DC, Congressional Research Service, 9 August 1994).

32 See John Borawski, 'Partnership for Peace and beyond', *International Affairs*, vol. 71, no. 2, April 1995, p. 242. On the importance of Polish and Czech pressure in pushing Clinton towards the idea of expansion see Joseph Fitchett, 'Moving Cautiously on NATO Expansion Eastward', *IHT*, 29 May 1995.

33 For a review of the American position see Stanley R. Sloan, 'US perspectives on NATO's future', *International Affairs*, vol. 71, no. 2, April 1995, pp. 217–31, and Robert E. Hunter, 'Enlargement: Part of a strategy for projecting stability into Central Europe', *NATO Review*, vol. 43, no. 3, May 1995, pp. 3–8.

34 Zbigniew Brzezinski, 'NATO – Expand or Die?', *NYT*, 28 December 1994.

35 Charles William Maynes, 'For NATO, Expansion Could Prove Fatal', *NYT*, 2 January 1995.

36 Fred C. Ikle, 'How To Ruin NATO', *NYT*, 11 January 1995.

37 See Michael E. Brown, 'The Flawed Logic of NATO Expansion', *Survival*, vol. 37, no. 1, Spring 1995, pp. 34–52.

38 Quoted in Craig R. Whitney, 'Expand NATO? Yes, Say Most Experts, but What Does the Public Think?', *NYT*, 10 February 1995.

39 See Robert E. Hunter, 'Enlargement: Part of a strategy for projecting stability into Central Europe', *NATO Review*, vol. 43, no. 3, May 1995, p. 7.

40 Following a meeting of NATO foreign ministers in Noordwijk in the Netherlands, Russia ended its five-month freeze of NATO by finally and formally agreeing to join the Partnership for Peace. However, speaking after the meeting on 31 May 1995, the Russian foreign minister, Andrei Kozyrev, warned the Alliance to drop proposals to expand its membership to the countries of Central and Eastern Europe. No doubt in an effort to reassure the Russians, a second document laying down a 'special relationship' between NATO and Russia was also approved. Kozyrev reiterated, however, that 'the attitude of Russia toward enlargement of NATO remains unchanged'. See 'NATO Lauds Russia On Security Pact', *IHT*, 31 May 1995; and Michael Evans, 'Moscow agrees to new security deal with Nato', *The Times*, 1 June 1995.

41 On 25 April 1995, the Under Secretary of Commerce for International Trade, Jeffrey Garten, agreed that the security 'glue' holding the US and Europe together had lost its strength, and that the old strategic relationship had 'not yet been replaced by an offsetting increase in deep linkages in economic and commercial matters with Brussels or the European Union'. See his 'The United States and Europe: New Opportunities and Strategies', USIS European Wireless File, 26 April 1995.
42 See Malcolm Rifkind, 'Need for an Atlantic Community to better reflect US–European relations', *NATO Review*, no. 2, March 1995, pp. 11–14.
43 See economic report discussed in *Atlantic Outlook*, no. 73, 22 July 1994, pp. 1–2.

Chapter 7: The United States meets the Pacific century

1 James Baker III, 'America in Asia: Emerging Architecture for a Pacific Community' *FA*, vol. 70, no. 5, Winter 1991–1992, pp. 3–4.
2 See William R. Nester, *Japan's Growing Power over East Asia and the World Economy: Ends and Means* (London, Macmillan, 1990), pp. 13–45.
3 Figure on US jobs quoted by Secretary of Defense William Perry, *U.S. Security Policy in Korea* (US Department of State Dispatch), 9 May 1994, vol. 5, no. 19, p. 275.
4 For official US figures see Committee on Armed Services, House of Representatives *Report of the Delegation to East Asia* (USGPO, Washington DC, 1993), pp. 2–3, and Committee on Foreign Affairs, House of Representatives *U.S.–Asia Economic Relations* (USGPO, Washington DC, 1993).
5 See evidence presented to the Committee on Armed Services, House of Representatives in *Regional Threats and Defense Options for the 1990s* (USGPO, Washington DC, 1993), p. 377.
6 See Huan Guocang, 'China's Opening to the World', *Problems of Communism*, vol. 35, November–December 1986, pp. 59–77.
7 On 31 March 1993 in his hearings before the Senate Foreign Relations Committee confirming him as Assistant Secretary of State for East Asia and Pacific Affairs, a confident and polished Winston Lord outlined ten major goals for American policy in Asia and the Pacific. These included, among other things, the forging of a fresh global partnership with Japan, erasing the nuclear threat on the Korean peninsula, ensuring that political openness in China caught up with economic reform, and normalizing US relations with Vietnam. Within fifteen months of Clinton taking office, relations between the US and East Asia had soured – as a later leaked memo from Winston Lord explained. The reason, according to Lord, was that Asians were 'beginning to resist the nature of that engagement'. Quote in Robert A. Manning and Paula Stern, 'The Myth of the Pacific Community',

FA, vol. 73, no. 6, November–December 1994, p. 86. For the full transcript of the original Winston Lord testimony I am indebted to the United States Information Service at the US Embassy in London. The precise title of his 1993 testimony was 'Elements of Democracy Necessary for Modernization'.

8 Manning and Stern, p. 80.

9 See Richard Holbrooke, 'Japan and the United States: Ending the Unequal Partnership', *FA*, vol. 70, no. 5, Winter 1991–1992, p. 47.

10 See, for example, Michael Richardson, 'U.S. Admiral Warns of China's Big New Navy', *IHT*, 8 March 1995.

11 See Gerald Segal, *China Changes Shape: Regionalism and Foreign Policy*, Adelphi Paper 287 (London, Brassey's, March 1994).

12 See the 'Special Report' of the North Korea Working Group of the United States Institute of Peace in *The Security Situation On The Korean Peninsula*. Committee On Foreign Affairs, House of Representatives, 24 February 1994 (USGPO, Washington DC, 1994).

13 See Kenichiro Sasae, *Rethinking Japan–US Relations*, Adelphi Paper 292 (London, Brassey's, December 1994), p. 33.

14 Secretary Baker, *A New Pacific Partnership: Framework for the Future*, Current Policy no. 1185 (USGPO, Washington DC, 26 June 1989).

15 See Robert Gilpin, *The Political Economy of International Relations* (Princeton University Press, 1987), pp. 317–39; C. Fred Bergsten, 'Economic Imbalances and World Politics', *FA*, vol. 64, no. 3, Spring 1987, pp. 790–93, and his 'The World Economy after the Cold War', *FA*, Summer 1990, vol. 69, no. 3, pp. 96–112; Zbigniew Brzezinski, 'How About an Informal U.S. Japan Inc.?', *NYT*, 28 April 1987.

16 Gerard Toal, 'The new East–West conflict? Japan and the Bush administration's "New World Order"', *Area*, vol. 25, no. 2, 1993, pp. 127–35.

17 Chalmers Johnson, *MITI and the Japanese Miracle* (Stanford, Stanford University Press, 1982), Karel Van Wolferen, *The Enigma of Japanese Power* (New York, Vintage, 1989), and James Fallows, *Looking at the Sun: the Rise of the New East Asian Economic and Political System* (New York, Pantheon Books, 1994). For an extremely sympathetic review of the Fallows volume see Chalmers Johnson, 'Intellectual Warfare', *Atlantic Monthly*, January 1995, pp. 99–104.

18 Roger C. Altman, 'Why Pressure Tokyo?', *FA*, vol. 73, no. 3, May–June 1994, p. 2.

19 For a critique of US trade policy see Jagdish Bhagwati, 'Samurais No More', *FA*, vol. 73, no. 3, May–June 1994, pp. 7–12.

20 See Andrew Pollack, 'U.S. Appears to Retreat From Setting Targets to Increase Japan's Imports', in *NYT*, 10 July 1993.

21 See David Sanger, 'Hosakawa's Move Foils U.S. Strategy', *IHT*, 11 April 1994; Nancy Dunne and Michito Nakamato, 'Wiser US to meet chastened

Japan', *FT*, 18 May 1994; and Reginald Dale, 'Japan Gains the Edge in Trade War', *IHT*, 13 September 1994.

22 'Defending trade', *FT*, 22 May 1995.

23 Quote from Guy de Jonquières, 'Japanese quietly celebrate world trade victory', *FT*, 20 March 1995.

24 Lionel Barber, 'EU backs Japan for UN role', *FT*, 9 March 1995.

25 David Dodwell, 'US economists attack "myopic" trade call', *FT*, 7 October 1993.

26 Quoted in Ramesh Ponnuru, *The Mystery of Japanese Growth*, Rochester Paper, No. 4 (London, Centre for Policy Studies, 1995).

27 Amongst the more vocal critics of Clinton's climbdown were Clyde V. Prestowitz Jr. and Alan Tonelson, 'All the Empty Threats Against Japan Have Gotten America Nowhere', *IHT*, 28 September 1994.

28 See Harry Harding in *The Future Of U.S. Foreign Policy (Part I): Regional Issues*. Hearings Before the Committee on Foreign Affairs, House of Representatives, 17 February 1993 (USGPO, Washington DC, 1993), pp. 360–80.

29 As suggested by Jim Mann and Art Pine in 'U.S. Plans First Port Call to China Since '89 Crackdown', *IHT*, 24 February 1995.

30 See Bill Bradley, 'Trade, the Real Engine of Democracy', *NYT*, 25 April 1994.

31 Trade figures from 'China wants to join the club', *Economist*, 14 May 1994, p. 83.

32 See Kevin Murphy, 'China Firms Learning to Play by Rules of the Game', *IHT*, 2 March 1995.

33 Quote from Daniel Williams, 'The Fits and Starts of U.S. China Ties', *IHT*, 14 February 1995.

34 David Shattuck, 'No Improvement In Human Rights In China In 1994', *Unofficial Transcript*, 2 February 1995, USIA Foreign Press Center briefing.

35 See, for example, Leslie Gelb, 'Asian Arms Races', *NYT*, 18 March 1993.

36 Tony Walker, 'Both living in interesting times', *FT*, 13 February 1995.

37 Richard L. Grant, 'China and Its Asian Neighbours: Looking Toward the Twenty First Century', *Washington Quarterly*, vol. 17, no. 1, Winter 1994, p. 61.

38 Leif R. Rosenberger, 'Unifying Korea: Beyond Hopes and Fears', *Contemporary Southeast Asia*, vol. 16, no. 3, December 1994, pp. 295–316.

39 For a different perspective on the likelihood of economic reform in North Korea see Byung-joon Ahn, 'The Man who would be Kim', *FA*, vol. 73, no. 6, November–December 1994, p. 98.

40 Quote from Thomas W. Lippmann, 'U.S. Considered Attacks on N. Korea, Perry Tells Panel', *Washington Post*, 25 January 1995.

41 The Scowcroft remarks were made on BBC radio, 21 March 1995.

42 Secretary of Defense William Perry, *U.S. Security Policy in Korea* (US Department of State Dispatch), 9 May 1994, vol. 5, no. 19.
43 'Statement by Secretary of State Warren Christopher before the Senate Foreign Relations Committee' (Department of State, Tuesday 24 January 1995).
44 Details of the agreement from Robert A. Manning, 'U.S. Policy Toward The Korean Peninsula: Beyond The Nuclear Accord', *Policy Briefing* (Washington DC, Progressive Policy Institute), 23 January 1995.
45 Paul D. Wolfowitz, 'The North Korea Deal Ignores Tension With The South', *IHT*, 25 February 1995.
46 See Jim Hoagland, 'North Korea: Washington Has Some Hard Selling to Do at Home', *IHT*, 6 December 1994.
47 My assessment of the ease with which the Clinton administration sold the nuclear agreement to Congress is based upon attendance at the Senate Hearings on Tuesday 24 January 1995. For an excellent discussion of the wider implications of the agreement see John Burton, 'The North–South divide narrows', *FT*, 24 October 1994.
48 See Neil Wilson, 'Enter a new dragon?', *The Banker*, April 1990, p. 26.
49 See Ron Moreau, 'Hello Vietnam', *Newsweek*, 10 June 1991, pp. 36–40; and Teresa Poole, 'Why Vietnam needs America', *Independent*, 30 December 1991.
50 Victor Mallet, 'Look east – but don't touch', *FT*, 16 September 1993.
51 For background on the US embargo (and its lifting) see Murray Hiebert and Susumu Awanohara, 'Lukewarm Welcome', *Far Eastern Economic Review*, 17 February 1994, pp. 14–15.
52 See Steven Greenhouse, 'U.S. Opens to Talks on Ties to Vietnam', *NYT*, 24 October 1991.
53 See Victor Mallet, 'Washington on defensive over loans for Vietnam', *FT*, 7 May 1993.
54 Quote from *NYT*, 4 February 1994.
55 See Jon Swain, 'The rich and the red chew the fat with Bill', *Sunday Times*, 21 November 1993.
56 Quoted in David E. Sanger, 'Clinton In Seattle For Pacific Talks To Seek Markets', *NYT*, 19 November 1993.
57 Ibid.
58 Quoted in Steven Greenhouse, 'Clinton Pushing Business With Asia', *NYT*, 11 November 1993.
59 See Fred Begsten, 'APEC and World Trade', *FA*, vol. 73, no. 3, May–June 1994, pp. 20–26.
60 See the essays on Asia-Pacific in *National Interest*, no. 38, Winter 1994–5, pp. 19–50.
61 According to Don Russell, Australian ambassador to the United States, APEC was 'an important device for keeping the US engaged in the

region'. Cited in Alexander Nicoll and George Graham, 'Hands across the water', *FT*, 15 November 1993.

62 See Manning and Stern, *FA*, p. 81.

63 Quote from Kazuo Ogura, Director-General of Economic Affairs at Japan's Foreign Ministry, *IHT*, 15 November 1993.

Chapter 8: Whatever happened to the Third World?

1 Quote from John F. Burns, 'As U.S. Aid Ends, Needs of Afghan War Victims Persists', *NYT*, 22 February 1995.

2 See Gabriel Kolko, *Confronting the Third World: United States Foreign Policy, 1945–1980* (New York, Knopf, 1988), and Peter Rodman, *More Precious Than Peace: The Cold War and the Struggle for the Third World* (New York, Charles Scribner's Sons, 1994).

3 See Peter J. Schraeder, '"It's the Third World stupid!" Why the Third World should be the priority of the Clinton administration', *Third World Quarterly*, vol. 14, no. 2, 1993, pp. 215–39.

4 See H.W. Brands, *The Specter of Neutralism: the United States and the Emergence of the Third World, 1947–1960* (New York, Columbia University Press, 1989).

5 See Melvyn Leffler, *A Preponderance of Power: National Security, the Truman Administration and the Cold War* (Stanford University Press, 1992), esp. pp. 164–72.

6 For the classic US statement on an economic agenda for the developing nations in the Cold War, see W.W. Rostow, *Stages of Economic Growth: A Non-Communist Manifesto* (Cambridge University Press, 1960).

7 See Kurt London, ed., *New Nations in a Divided World* (New York, Praeger Publishers, 1964).

8 See Michael Cox, 'The Soviet–American Conflict in the Third World', in Peter Shearman and Phil Williams, eds, *The Superpowers, Central America and the Middle East* (London, Brassey's Defence Publishers, 1988), pp. 171–85.

9 See Bruce D. Porter, *The USSR In Third World Conflicts: Soviet Arms and Diplomacy in Local Wars: 1945–1980* (Cambridge University Press, 1984).

10 See John Dumbrell, *The Carter Presidency: A re-evaluation* (Manchester University Press, 1993), esp. pp. 110–209.

11 Fred Halliday, *Cold War, Third World* (London, Hutchinson Radius, 1989), p. 29.

12 Quote in Clyde H. Farnsworth, 'Conable's World Bank: Finding Fault and Praise', *NYT*, 1 February 1990.

13 See President Reagan, 'America's Foreign Policy Challenges for the 1980s' (Washington, Department of State, 6 April 1984).

14 On the end of apartheid see the essays collected by Jack Spence in his indispensable edited volume, *Change in South Africa* (London, Pinter/RIIA, 1994).
15 See Nigel Harris, *The End of the Third World* (London, Penguin Books, 1990).
16 See Robert W. Tucker and David C. Hendrickson, *The Imperial Temptation* (New York, Council on Foreign Relations Press, 1992).
17 James Petras and Steve Vieux, 'The Decline of Revolutionary Politics: Capitalist Detour and the Return of Socialism', *Journal of Contemporary Asia*, vol. 24, no. 1, 1994, pp. 29–33.
18 On US policy in Somalia see *Operation Restore Hope: A Document Collection* (The Reference Center, United States Information Service, Embassy of America, London, 1992). For two excellent critiques of US policy see Theo Farrell, 'Explaining the Failure Of the US Intervention In Somalia: Military Culture, Organization and Knowledge', Paper presented at the American Politics Group of the PSA Annual Conference, 4–6 January 1995, and M.M. Sahnoun, 'Prevention in conflict resolution: the case of Somalia', *Irish Studies In International Affairs*, vol. 5, 1994, pp. 5–13.
19 See See Michael R. Gordon, 'U.S. Acting More Urgently To End Rwanda Slaughter', *NYT*, 16 June 1994.
20 See 'Still A U.S. Invasion. Still Wrong', *NYT*, 2 September 1994, and Jeanne Kirkpatrick, 'Imposing Democracy: Could U.S. Stop With Haiti?', *IHT*, 10–11 September 1994.
21 Peter Rodman, 'The Risks Mount Up For Clinton', *IHT*, 19 September 1994.
22 See 'Challenging U.S. Policy Toward Africa: Conversations with Randall Robinson', *Journal of International Affairs*, Summer 1992, vol. 46, no. 1, pp. 145–56.
23 See *Development And Democracy In Africa*, Hearing Before the Subcommittee On Africa Of The Committee On Foreign Affairs, House of Representatives, 22 April 1993 (USGPO, Washington DC, 1994), p. 95.
24 Peter J. Schraeder, *United States Foreign Policy Toward Africa: Incrementalism, Crisis and Change* (Cambridge University Press, 1994), p. 250.
25 Ibid., p. 251.
26 While US aid fell, the African debt as a whole rose from \$122.4bn in 1982 to \$235.6bn in 1991. As of 1990, sub-Saharan Africa owed \$161bn, primarily to official bilateral and multilateral sources. Figures from Darryl C. Thomas and Ali A. Mazrui, 'Africa's Post-Cold War Demilitarization: Domestic and Global Causes', *Journal of International Affairs*, Summer 1992, vol. 46, no. 1, p. 171, and Michael Chege, 'Remembering Africa', *FA*, vol. 71, no. 1, 1992, p. 156.
27 On declining African trade figures, see *Africa, Make or Break: Action for Recovery* (Oxford, Oxfam Publications, 1993).

28 See *The Season of Peace: The Israel–Palestinian Accord and the U.S. Commitment to the Middle East Process*, United States Information Agency, February 1994.
29 Figures from Carroll J. Doherty, 'Stalemate Stalls President's Overhaul of Foreign Aid', *Congressional Quarterly*, 2 April 1994, p. 808.
30 For historical background see Howard J. Wiarda, *American Foreign Policy Toward Latin America in the 80s and 90s* (New York University Press, 1992).
31 See, for example, Jorge G. Castaneda, *Utopia Unarmed: The Latin American Left After the Cold War* (New York, Knopf, 1993).
32 See Richard E. Feinberg, Special Assistant to the president for Inter-American Affairs, National Security Council, *Substantive Symmetry in Hemispheric Relations* (US Department of State Dispatch), 14 March 1994, vol. 5, no. 11.
33 See Alexander F. Watson, Assistant Secretary for Inter-American Affairs, *Key Issues in Inter-American Relations* (US Department of State Dispatch), 17 January 1994, vol. 5, no. 3.
34 Latin America (and the Caribbean), however, were the hardest hit of any Third World region in terms of US aid reductions; for the financial years 1994 and 1995 aid declined by nearly 50 per cent. Ibid., p. 26.
35 'New friends, new ideas', *Guardian*, 14 May 1995.
36 See Jim Hoagland, 'How Pakistan Helped Iran, and Clinton Alerted Yeltsin', *IHT*, 18 May 1995.
37 Tom Rhodes, 'Bhutto insists US deliver warplanes or hand back $1bn', *The Times*, 11 April 1995.
38 Tim McGirk, 'Washington woos India as Cold War ends', *Independent*, 16 November 1991. On the economic background to the 1991 decision to reform the Indian economy see Bimal Jalan, *India's Economic Crisis: The Way Ahead* (Oxford University Press, 1991).
39 See Nancy Dunne, 'US tries to melt the ice with India', *FT*, 6 April 1994, and Stefan Wagstyl, 'Rao tries to build bridges to Washington', *FT*, 13 May 1994.
40 Mark Nicholson, 'Fears grow over US investment in India', *FT*, 16 June 1995, and his 'The politics of Indian power', *FT*, 20 June 1995. See also 'Maharastra', *FT Survey*, 19 June 1995, pp. 1, 6.
41 'India and America: Looking for friends', *Economist*, 21 May 1994.
42 See Selig S. Harrison, 'Let's Get Off the Road to Nuclear War in South Asia', *IHT*, 4 March 1992, and Sumit Ganguly and Mitchell Reiss, 'The Subcontinent Doesn't Need Indian Ballistic Missiles', *IHT*, 7 September 1994.
43 See Keith Griffin, 'Foreign Aid after the Cold War', *Development and Change*, vol. 22, no. 4, October 1991, pp. 645–86.
44 See 'Why aid is an empty promise', *Economist*, 7 May 1994, pp. 13–14, 21–26.

45 See *Overview of Foreign Assistance*, Hearings Before the Subcommittee on International Economic Policy, Trade, Oceans and Environment of the Committee on Foreign Relations, United States Senate (USGPO, Washington DC, 1991), and Ernest Graves, 'Restructuring Foreign Assistance', *Washington Quarterly*, Summer 1993, pp. 189–98.
46 See *Foreign Aid Reform*, Hearings Before the Committee on Foreign Affairs, House of Representatives, 26 July 1993 (USGPO, Washington DC, 1993).
47 See Deputy Secretary Wharton, *USAID and Foreign Aid Reform*, US Department of State Dispatch, 26 July 1993, vol. 4, no. 30.
48 See *Foreign Assistance Legislation For Fiscal Year 1994 (Part 3)*, Hearing Before the Subcommittee on Economic Policy and Environment of the Committee on Foreign Affairs, House of Representatives (USGPO, 4 and 12 May 1993).
49 On 11 May 1995 the Senate and House Budget Committees recommended sharp cuts in foreign aid spending. The Senate version would have reduced USAID spending by $2.7bn over five years and foreign aid spending overall by $18.1bn between 1996 and 2002. In the House version, overall foreign aid would be reduced by $29bn over the same period. See 'Foreign Aid Faces Stiffest Challenge Yet in Congress', in *Atlantic Outlook*, no. 85, 19 May 1995, p. 4. See also Barbara Crossette, 'Foreign Aid Budget: Quick, How Much? Wrong', *NYT*, 27 February 1995.
50 'The question of foreign aid', *U.S. News & World Report*, 30 January 1995.
51 See James C. Clad and Roger D. Stone, 'New Mission For Foreign Aid', *FA*, vol. 72, no. 1, Spring 1993, pp. 196–205.
52 See *The Earth Summit: One Year On*, House of Commons Library, Research Paper 93/71, 25 June 1993.
53 For US reservations about the Rio Declaration see David Lascelles and Christina Lamb, 'Protection of bio-diversity sparks Rio controversy', and David Lascelles, 'Showpiece document pleases nobody much', *FT*, 8 June 1992. See also the special section on 'The Earth Summit', *FT*, 11 June 1992.
54 See Al Gore, *Earth in the Balance: Forging a new Common Purpose* (London, Earthscan, 1992).
55 My discussion here draws on Ian H. Rowlands, 'Achieving Sustainable Development: getting a good thing', *Third Word Quarterly*, vol. 14, no. 2, 1993, pp. 385–92.
56 See *Statement of Glenn T. Prickett*, Before the Subcommittee on Economic Policy, Trade and Environment, Committee on Foreign Affairs, U.S. House of Representatives, 4 May 1993 (National Resource Defense Council, Washington DC).
57 See also Mark Curtis, 'West European Security and the Third World', in

Mark Curtis et al., *Challenges and Responses to Future European Security: British, French and German Perspectives* (European Strategy Group, 1993), pp. 69–111.

Chapter 9: Conclusion

1 See Benjamin Schwarz, 'America's Global Role In The Post-Cold War Period'. Paper presented to the Conference 'Kennan, the Cold War, and the Future of American Foreign Policy', The School of International Relations, Center for International Studies of the University of Southern California, 27–29 January 1995.

2 See Ronald Steel, 'Internationalism as a Complement to Nationalism', *IHT*, 8 June 1995.

3 See Michael Cox, 'From the Truman Doctrine to the Second Superpower Detente: The Rise and Fall of the Cold War', *Journal of Peace Research*, vol. 27, no. 1, 1990, pp. 25–41; and 'From Detente to the "New Cold War": The Crisis of the Cold War System', *Millennium*, vol. 13, no. 3, Winter 1984, pp. 265–91.

4 Jim Hoagland, 'Signs of a Global Decline in America's Ability to Command Respect', *IHT*, 21 May 1995. See also the comments by Jack Spence on the 'travails of a superpower' in his 'Entering the future backwards: some reflections on the current international scene', *Review of International Studies*, vol. 20, 1994, pp. 11–12.